W9-CBW-571

Other Jossey-Bass Titles on Board Leadership

Boards That Make a Difference, Second Edition, *John Carver*

Reinventing Your Board, *John Carver, Miriam Mayhew Carver*

John Carver on Board Leadership

Corporate Boards That Create Value, *John Carver with Caroline Oliver*

The CarverGuides 1–12, *John Carver, Miriam Mayhew Carver:*

The Policy Governance Fieldbook, *Caroline Oliver*

John Carver on Board Governance, A Video Presentation

Empowering Boards for Leadership (audiotape), *John Carver*

Board Leadership: Policy Governance in Action (newsletter), *John Carver*

The Board Member's Playbook

The Board Member's Playbook

Using Policy Governance
to Solve Problems,
Make Decisions, and
Build a Stronger Board

Miriam Carver

Bill Charney

Foreword by John Carver

JOSSEY-BASS
A Wiley Imprint
www.josseybass.com

Library of Congress Cataloging-in-Publication Data
Carver, Miriam Mayhew.
  The board member's playbook : using policy governance to solve
problems, make decisions, and build a stronger board / Miriam Carver,
Bill Charney ; foreword by John Carver.-1st ed.
      p. cm.
Includes bibliographical references.
  ISBN 0-7879-6840-4 (alk. paper)
  1. Boards of directors. 2. Corporate governance. I. Title: Board
member's play book. II. Charney, Bill. III. Title.
  HD2745.C375 2004
  658.4'012-dc22
                                                2003019387

Printed in the United States of America

FIRST EDITION

PB Printing   10 9 8 7 6 5 4 3 2 1

Contents

Rehearsal Scenarios

Foreword

THE POLICY GOVERNANCE® MODEL introduced a new and demanding level of excellence to boards of directors. Because it is demanding—and because it differs radically from the conventional wisdom—the model is not for everyone. It is not that the model fails to apply to all governing boards but rather that not all board members have or even aspire to the patience for the rigorous board leadership the model both demands and enables. For those who do—or who are interested in what it might mean—there is now *The Board Member's Playbook* to help them fulfill the commendable commitment they have already made.

It seems deceptively simple, but one of the core problems of boards is their failure to use any coherent system of governance at all. Most board life consists of a constant stream of decisions to be made or, more accurately, approvals to be granted. Although boards differ in how much attention they give to these decision events (from blithe rubber-stamping to painstaking pursuit of trivia), they are alike in being driven by whatever fate throws their way. It is as if boards are being governed—if not by troublesome incidents, then by their own staffs—instead of governing. Real leaders get in front of the parade, and that requires a systematic approach capable of embracing events rather than being driven by them. There is merit in knowing that when dilemmas do arise, there is an organized, carefully considered, values-based way not only to solve them but also to move beyond them. Maintaining such exemplary leadership requires *practice.*

The concept of organized, frequent board practice may have an unfamiliar ring. My first encounter with the idea was Miriam Carver's presentation to a symposium of Policy Governance consultants in 2001. As she and Bill Charney point out in these pages, everyone understands that performers of any sort (musicians, athletes, soldiers) must practice far more than they perform. And the need is even more pronounced in the case of group performance, for interpersonal interaction is added to—or rather becomes an integral and complicated part of—basic skill development. The surprising thing is not that there is now a book on governance rehearsals but that the idea strikes us as novel. That fact is truly a diagnostic comment on the widespread lack of rigor usually brought to the board task.

For me, the value in this book lies in its very concrete, step-by-step counsel to boards about how to capitalize on the idea of practice. The prescriptions Miriam and Bill so logically lay out are consistent with and built firmly on good theory, to be sure, and that is why the practical part is so, well, practical. Board members drawn to the conceptual coherence of the Policy Governance model can follow the authors' specific instructions knowing that model consistency has been carefully built in.

What benefits should a board expect from the authors' recommendations? Added to what the authors quite adequately answer with respect to this question, here are the benefits that strike me as important.

• *Rehearsals supply a mechanism to keep the board on its toes.* Boards that adopt Policy Governance, even those that never get around to fulfilling their all-important Ends obligation, find that crises diminish or disappear and the seduction into micromanagement vanishes. While those are great benefits, a board that previously felt as if it were shooting the rapids can become complaisant in the new calm waters. A more leisurely boardroom ambiance risks becoming one of carelessness or even negligence. Rehearsals enable a board to stay sharp without courting disaster to do it.

• *Rehearsals bolster the realism of a "virtual boss" for a group of equals.* It is no secret that groups without an authoritative leader have a hard time being responsible. Yet that is exactly the situation with boards, where the group *as a group* is the seat of authority. It is typical for boards to disregard their group duty by allowing the chief governance officer (CGO) or chief executive officer (CEO) to become the boss. The Policy Governance model doesn't allow a board to cheat its obligation to be an authoritative owner-representative, so the board must find a way to be disciplined and wise as a group in the absence of an on-site superior. The board's obligation is to the owners, of course, but owners are neither on-site nor unified in their opinions and expressions. So in practice, the board works for the "virtual boss" of its own group commitment. Although the CGO can surely be the board's chief guardian of board discipline, the source of authority is not the CGO at all but the rules the board has accepted for itself. Rehearsals afford a way for that virtual boss (the set of principles to which the board is committed) to acquire a persistent and forceful in-your-face reality.

- *Rehearsals provide concrete lessons to new members.* A board might spend months learning Policy Governance and require even longer for the new discipline to feel natural. Curiously, the same board might thoughtlessly pop a new member into this new and unfamiliar world with, at best, a short orientation. The new board member must learn largely from watching the behavior of more experienced colleagues. Rehearsals, because they organize that learning more pointedly, promise to get the new member up to speed faster than if he or she were exposed only to the unhurried, normal flow of board issues. It is very instructive to experience how to handle a crisis before one occurs.

Governing boards are still the least developed element in enterprise. But progress is being made among boards bold enough and committed enough to demand of themselves sound performance built on credible theory. Realistic guides like *The Board Member's Playbook*—the ninth book to be published on the theory or implementation of the Policy Governance model—may well be the most crucial remaining ingredient in an eventual triumph of superior governance. Miriam Carver and Bill Charney, by contributing this highly practical guide to the literature, make it more possible that boards committed to excellence can actually attain and maintain it.

November 2003   JOHN CARVER
                                                        Atlanta, Georgia

John Carver, Ph.D., is the creator of the Policy Governance model, widely considered the world's only coherent theory of governance. He is author or coauthor of five books, fourteen monographs, over 170 published articles, and various electronic materials on the topic and has consulted on six continents. He holds adjunct professorships at the University of Georgia Institute for Nonprofit Organizations in Athens, Georgia, and the Schulich School of Business at York University in Toronto, Ontario, Canada.

Preface

BOARDS OF DIRECTORS are routinely confronted by challenges and questions. Often they encounter difficulty arriving at an answer, perhaps because there seem to be so many reasonable alternatives, or maybe because all the answers seem unsatisfactory. Sometimes boards decide that the answer is best left to others to find. Sometimes they try to answer the questions themselves. It's always a challenge at the board table to decide not only how to answer questions but also what questions to answer.

It helps if the board is using a framework that guides its decision making.

The Policy Governance model is such a framework. It allows boards to govern according to their values as expressed in policies. These policies outline the board's rules for itself as well as for everyone who works for the board. Of primary importance is that they address the purpose the board expects the organization to fulfill and the rules guiding the prudence and ethics of decision making.

Even when using a governance operating system like Policy Governance, organizing the board's work and recognizing decision-making roles is difficult. Having policies is an important first step, but using them well is necessary also. We wrote this book because we are absolutely sure that good rehearsal will result in the building of good board skills. Feedback from our colleagues has reinforced this view. Miriam Carver developed the concept driving this book and presented it at a Policy Governance conference in 2001. The idea was warmly received; others could easily see how helpful governance rehearsal would be in the building of board skills. Many consultants expressed the hope that the idea would be presented in book form.

The Board Member's Playbook is intended to be helpful for several types of readers. First, members of Policy Governance boards will find it useful to review the Policy Governance model and to complete the rehearsal exercises using their policies as a guide. We expect that increased confidence and skill in the use of Policy Governance will result. Second, members of boards not using Policy Governance will have an opportunity to learn about this increasingly well known system, as well as to experience how an operating template will simplify the problems of deciding who does what in an organization. Third, Policy Governance consultants will have at their disposal a teaching tool that helps make real the concepts that their client boards struggle to learn and put into practice. Fourth, for board members who are interested in finding solutions to problems commonly encountered in the boardroom, the completed worksheets in Part Two of the book will be a valuable resource.

How to Use This Book and the Accompanying CD-ROM

Part One allows us to share with you our thinking about the importance of rehearsal to successful governance. We encourage you to read Chapter One in order to understand why we describe boards of directors as groups of individuals that must strive to perform effectively as teams. You will read about the perils of failing to rehearse as well as the benefits gained by boards that do use this skill-building method. Chapter Two outlines the process of governance rehearsal itself and offers some pointers designed to help you get the most out of the rehearsal exercises.

Part Two is where you do the work. Chapters Three through Six contain a range of rehearsal scenarios and worksheets we have designed to guide you through the steps of problem solving. If you are on a Policy Governance board, we encourage you to use your board policy manual as a reference in resolving the scenarios. As an alternative, you may choose to use the set of sample policies we have included in this book (see Resource 3). These chapters also contain our responses to the rehearsal scenarios so that you can compare your responses to ours.

The book ends with four useful "resources." Resource 1 presents an overview of the Policy Governance model. This will come in handy for readers who wish to review the model's principles and will be especially instructive for readers who are not yet acquainted with Policy Governance.

In Resource 2, we provide a rehearsal worksheet that can be copied and used in your rehearsals. This same worksheet is found on the accompanying CD-ROM; you can print and save the worksheet on your computer. Resource 3 ("A Sample Board Policy Manual") provides a set of sample policies, including generic policies used by Policy Governance boards regarding Executive Limitations, the Governance Process, and Board-Management Delegation, as well as sample Ends policies relevant to organizations of a variety of types. The sample policy manual is present also on the CD-ROM, along with our responses to each of the rehearsal scenarios found in the worksheets in Chapters Three through Six. In these responses (on the CD-ROM), policy reference numbers are *indexed* (linked) to the corresponding policies in the sample manual: When you click your mouse on a policy number in a worksheet, your screen will switch over to the policy manual and your cursor will appear at the corresponding policy. This indexing feature will aid you in referring back and forth to the sample policy manual as you read the worksheet responses. You will find also on the CD-ROM the blank worksheet for each rehearsal scenario.

Finally, in Resource 4, we provide a list of suggestions for further reading.

We are grateful for the opportunity to work with you and your board in fine-tuning your Policy Governance skills. We hope our format works well for you.

Naturally, using any format, even using it well, does not guarantee wisdom of content. That we leave to you!

November 2003   MIRIAM CARVER
                                                       Atlanta, Georgia

                                                       BILL CHARNEY
                                                       Denver, Colorado

Acknowledgments

WE ARE SO GRATEFUL to John Carver for creating the Policy Governance model in the first place, for if the theory were not so rich, there would be little point in pursuing ways to perfect its use.

Many of our colleagues who are Policy Governance consultants and many of our clients assisted us by sharing their struggles with attaining governance excellence. We are grateful for their generosity and encouragement. In particular, the colleagues and clients who gave us material for the rehearsal scenarios were Jan Adelman, Jim Baldwin, Linda Bestimt, Linda Childears, Dick Clark, Bob D'Alessandro, Ron Gager, Elaine Harrington, Tyler Lantzy, Reid Lehman, Judy Levesque, Roger Neeland, Caroline Oliver, Judy Osbourne, Jan Rhode, Liz Schrader, Bruce Skinner, and Lynn Walker. We greatly appreciate their contributions.

Numerous other people also helped us write this book. Caroline Oliver was very instrumental in the development of the worksheets used in the book. We thank our editor, Dorothy Hearst, who encouraged, challenged, and guided us through the process.

John Carver reviewed the manuscript and gave us a great deal of very useful assistance, for which we are deeply indebted. And Ivan Benson, as always, contributed his organizational skills to our great benefit.

Finally, we thank our long-suffering families, John Carver, Betty Charney, and Anna and Aaron Charney, for putting up with us while we wrote this book.

M.C., B.C.

The Authors

MIRIAM CARVER is a Policy Governance consultant and presenter, as well as a trainer of Policy Governance consultants, co-teaching (with Dr. John Carver) the Policy Governance Academy, in which consultants learn theoretical and application skills. For more than a decade, she has worked with boards and presented to audiences in the United States, Canada, Great Britain, and Continental Europe. She has facilitated Policy Governance implementation with boards of nonprofit, governmental, for-profit, and cooperative organizations and enjoys coaching managers who work for these boards. Carver was raised in England and after obtaining her bachelor of arts degree moved to Canada, where she earned her master's degree. Her CEO experience was gained first as executive director of Canada's first AIDS hospice and then as executive director of a trade association of counseling agencies. Carver has coauthored two previous books, four booklets in the Jossey-Bass CarverGuide series, and a number of articles dealing with the Policy Governance model of board leadership. She bases her consulting practice in Atlanta, Georgia, where she lives with her husband, Dr. John Carver, the originator of the Policy Governance model. Miriam Carver can be reached at (404) 728-0091; fax: (404) 728-0060: e-mail: miriamcarver@miriamcarver.com; Web site: http://www.miriamcarver.com

BILL CHARNEY is a consultant, speaker, and trainer in board governance and leadership. Personally selected and trained by Dr. John Carver, Charney has particular expertise in helping boards elevate effectiveness and accountability using the Policy Governance model. After earning his M.B.A. in organization management from the University of Colorado, Charney founded and, as CEO, led Denver's Cherry Creek Arts Festival to acclaim as one of the world's most respected festival organizations and the top ranking among U.S. visual arts festivals. He chaired the board of directors of the International Festivals and Events Association, was elected by peers to be a founding board member of the International Policy Governance Association, and has served on numerous other boards. As a consultant and speaker, he has assisted hundreds of boards and CEOs in defining roles, authority, and accountability and has provided policy development assistance to a wide variety of nonprofit, public, and corporate boards. Charney lives with his wife, Betty, and their twins, Anna and Aaron, in Denver, Colorado. He can be reached at (303) 321-3190; on the Web at http://www.bcharney.com; or via e-mail at bill@bcharney.com

Part One

The Need for Board Rehearsal

THE FIRST CHAPTER of this book introduces you to the idea of board rehearsal and explains why it is so important for board success. Then, in the second chapter, we outline the rehearsal method we have developed and show you how to use our rehearsal worksheets.

Chapter 1

Board Rehearsal: Why?

VIRTUALLY EVERYWHERE in society we encounter organizations that have boards. Corporations have boards. We elect boards to govern our counties, cities, and schools. Boards lead professional societies and trade associations. And boards govern a huge array of nonprofit organizations, including those involved in health, human services, and the arts. Clearly, the job of a board is of immense social and economic importance.

But what makes for an effective board? Is a board simply as good as the people who are on it? Should it be better than the sum of its parts? Or is it, curiously, sometimes worse?

Governing boards are groups with a job to do. They are not mere figureheads, nor are they just pools of operational volunteers. The board's job is to govern the organization and ensure its accountable performance.

For other groups that must achieve success as a group, two conditions must be met. These conditions apply to boards too. The first condition is that the requirements or expectations of the group job must be clear. Without clear requirements or rules, groups become confused about their job. They often end up defining their job by default as whatever their individual members want to do. The second condition is that the skills and behaviors required to meet the expectations must be rehearsed.

The Necessity for Clear Expectations

Whenever a job requires the work of more than one person, coordination of effort is essential. Multiple players present numerous opportunities for mistakes, misunderstandings, and failures. Groups, whether they are sports teams, orchestras, military units, flight deck crews, or governing boards, are by their very nature vulnerable to such risks.

A key to success is the existence of expectations and rules not just about what group members are to do in "normal" circumstances but also about what is to be done when the unanticipated occurs.

The initial step is to define positions clearly. Who is supposed to be where? What roles are team members supposed to play? How much authority do they have over others? For a sports team, specific positions are usually well defined and understood. In a flight crew, a pilot and first officer have clearly defined roles, positions, and authority. In the context of the board of directors, there must be clarity about where the board fits relative to the other parts of the organization. There must be a clear understanding about the authority of the board and what this means about the authority of its individual members.

The next step is to clarify what people are to do in their respective positions. For symphonies, the musical score maps this out. Flight crews have clearly defined operating procedures. For sports teams, a document outlining specific intended actions is often called a "playbook." Playbooks map out the proactive plays the team plans to initiate and utilize. Playbooks also outline the defensive actions and options available when it is necessary to react, whether to external circumstances (what the other team does) or to the need for internal backup and support (for example, if a team member for some reason fails to do what is expected). For boards, there must be clear expectations about what the board decides, what board members are required to do to contribute to the board's own work, and what is left to others to decide. These expectations should be as useful when the unanticipated occurs as when all goes as planned.

The Importance of Rehearsal to Skill Development

Repetition of a skill is fundamental to improving or even maintaining performance. It is undeniable that an individual's performance of cognitive skills (such as speaking a foreign language) or physical skills (such as dancing) will improve if the skill is repeated and practiced.

Rehearsal is as important in the building of group skills as it is in the development of individual skills. Indeed, recognizing the importance of rehearsal, many groups, such as orchestras, sports teams, and armies, spend more time practicing than actually performing. This rehearsal is important even if each member of the group is, as an individual, highly skilled in playing his or her part. After all, a symphony orchestra that hasn't rehearsed together probably won't sound its best, regardless of the number of virtuoso musicians on stage, and a cast of actors must rehearse no matter how many Oscar winners are among their number.

Practice for Boards

When a group has reached agreement regarding its purpose and process and has clarified its rules and expectations, it must practice how to work together. In this regard, boards of directors are not different from other groups. They need to rehearse how to work together in a way that is consistent with the rules they have established for themselves. This is especially important since boards have a great deal of authority and since other people depend on them to be fair and predictable.

It is important to note that governance rehearsal can be a meaningful concept only if the expectations and requirements of a governing board are clearly articulated. In other words, boards must rehearse in order to be effective, but unless there are established rules and expectations, *there is nothing to be rehearsed.* Accordingly, for many boards, the concept of rehearsal can be of no practical help until they have first decided and articulated their operating principles.

This book is addressed to boards that have operating principles whose use can be rehearsed. In particular, we are addressing governing boards that use or are considering using the Policy Governance model. These boards may be governing nonprofit, for-profit, cooperative, or governmental organizations. We advocate for this approach because Policy Governance boards have clearly articulated expectations of board position, performance, and authority. We will refer to these expectations as *policies.* We are assuming that readers have some familiarity with this widely used model, so we will use terminology specific to it. For example, the policies that describe the expectations of the board are referred to as *Governance Process* and *Board-Management Delegation* policies, and we will use these terms. If you are not familiar with the Policy Governance model, or if you want a refresher on its principles, you will find a summary of the model in Resource 1.

Policy Governance is a system that gives boards the tools it needs to establish the keys to group effectiveness. First, its use allows the board to spell out its rules and expectations for itself, as well as for those who report to it. These rules provide the board with the clarity we have described as essential to group success. They are in effect the board team's "playbook." Second, its use defines the board job clearly enough to allow the rehearsal of the skills and decision-making principles demanded by that job. After all, having a good playbook is important, but practicing how to use it is the essential second step. This book will show you how the board can rehearse by referring to its own policies to determine its response to problems or dilemmas.

When Boards Don't Rehearse

Since boards occupy the most authoritative position in organizations, they must accept the responsibility that accompanies their position. It is easy for board members to underestimate the board's power and influence and to forget that both board action and board inaction will have a ripple effect throughout the entire organization. Boards can easily acquire the reputation among the staff of being fickle, unpredictable, and even capricious. Many boards are simply regarded as irrelevant. Commonly, this perception is based on the observation that the board, even when it has made policies, ignores them, telegraphing that policies are to be disregarded. Staff often observes that the board uses its authority to make judgments of staff performance in the complete absence of preexisting criteria, telegraphing that unfairness is a threat. They see the board serially delegating and then undelegating responsibilities, causing confusion about who has authority and for what and telegraphing that confusion and frustration can be expected.

Clearly, the risks of unrehearsed governance practice can be huge. The board is, after all, a group that has authority over the entire organization and accountability for the organization's successes and failures. This group can cause the organization it governs to be entirely unclear about the expectations it must meet or the authority that has been delegated to meet them. It can cause the staff to be unsure about reporting lines and the CEO to be held accountable for decisions made not by the CEO but by the board itself. Indeed, it can seem to expect more disciplined behavior and performance of the staff than it does of itself. Without rehearsal, the board can find that the exigencies of today trump its necessary focus on the future, and it may find that without practiced adherence to its own policies, its actual topics for discussion and decision making become merely a laundry list of the interests of its members.

When Boards Do Rehearse

Surprisingly, governance rehearsal is not a common feature of board agendas, even though we know that groups cannot perform well without practice. Even Policy Governance boards often fail to rehearse the method they decided to use, endangering their ability to use it.

But when Policy Governance boards do conduct rehearsals, numerous benefits accrue. First, the board that systematically refers to its policies prior to making a decision can avoid spending time on decisions it already made. Second, it can actually see that its policies have covered all organizational issues at some level. Third, it can quickly get to the heart of the matter that has come before the board. Fourth, it can understand clearly the nature of the decisions that it must make as well as those it should not make. Fifth, the power of its own words is evident to the board itself and to the staff, and the process of its decision making can be explained to others. Sixth, referring to standards of performance can protect against conflicts of interest and caprice. And finally, the board confirms that rigorous monitoring of its organization is absolutely essential.

It would be disingenuous if we did not point out some of the more difficult results of rehearsal. We have found that when a board systematically refers to its own policies to resolve problems, it sometimes uncovers that the problem has been caused by its own failure to abide by its word. If the board as a body or individual members of the board fail to live up to expectations, there can be no solution unless the board is willing to confront its own lapse. This means that the board must note its deviation from its own policies, correct the situation, and affirm its commitment to its own discipline.

For example, board rehearsal will press the board to lay aside personal negative opinions about a CEO whose performance is shown to meet expectations. Conversely, it will show that the board, despite its personal positive opinions, must deal with a popular but chronically failing CEO. Both situations are awkward to handle and tempting to avoid, and boards are as susceptible as any group to the impulse to gloss over problems. So the rehearsal of board discipline and consistency makes it hard to avoid dealing directly with problems, even when peers cause them.

Summary

The level of rigor and exactness required of a Policy Governance board is far greater than that achieved or even attempted in most boardrooms. Accordingly, the correct use of the Policy Governance model demands that the board pay close attention to its own behavior and job performance. Since the board using Policy Governance has expressed its expectations of its organization and itself in policy, solutions to boardroom dilemmas are to be found in the policy manual. The purpose of governance rehearsal, therefore, is to build board skill in referring to and acting in accordance with already articulated standards. Rehearsal is a process that allows the Policy Governance board to practice the skills required to make decisions consistent with the principles to which it has committed itself in Board-Management Delegation and Governance Process policies. In addition, it enables the board to reexamine and if necessary revise policies in order to guide future decision making.

Chapter 2

Board Rehearsal: How?

ALL PROBLEM SOLVING at the board level can and should begin with the board referring to its policy manual. Remember that *all* issues are addressed at some level of specificity in a manual based on the Policy Governance principles. This is the great advantage of using Policy Governance's exhaustive ends-means distinction and of deciding issues at the broadest level first, further defining them until any reasonable interpretation would be acceptable. Thus the first question to be asked by a board when it is confronted with a dilemma should be not "What should we do?" but rather "What have we already said about this?" When the board refers to its policies first, it will commonly find that the solution to the dilemma has already been addressed satisfactorily in policy. In this case, the board has nothing to do but follow its policy. It is relieved of the unnecessary work of trying to answer questions that have already been addressed and thus require no more time. Sometimes the board may find that its current policy on the topic at hand is one it wishes to further refine or change altogether. Amending the policies, if necessary, preserves their relevance and helps ensure that the organization and the board itself operate in accordance with up-to-date statements of board values. In addition, the board will be able to recognize issues that it has already delegated to another party, for example, the CEO. Accordingly, it will avoid the common practice of deciding issues that the CEO has already been authorized to decide.

How Often Should a Board Rehearse?

We strongly urge our clients and our readers to make rehearsal a regular part of their board meetings. Since the point of rehearsal is to build board skill, practicing on a regular and frequent basis makes a good deal of sense, especially as board composition changes due to turnover. Accordingly, we suggest that boards set aside a brief period of time during each board meeting to solve a scenario presented either in this book or by a board member, staff member, or any interested party. We urge boards to learn the method we will outline and to use it during their governance rehearsals. It should not take more than fifteen to twenty minutes to complete a rehearsal.

Who Should Lead the Rehearsal?

Boards differ in their answers to this question. Often the chair (whom we will refer to as the chief governance officer, or CGO, for reasons explained in Resource 1) is the best board member to lead the discussion. It is almost certainly the case that boards will expect their CGO to ensure that their intention to rehearse is actually carried out. The CGO may, however, decide to delegate to another board member the job of actually setting up and leading the exercise. Whoever is the most likely to helpfully lead the rehearsal should be the person to do it.

The Rehearsal Tool Kit

This workbook provides four tools to assist boards to rehearse: scenarios, worksheets, a policy manual, and our own worksheet responses.

Scenarios

We encourage boards or individual board members embarking on governance rehearsal to learn the method by using the fifty scenarios provided in Chapters Three through Six. The chapters contain rehearsal scenarios that describe problems that boards commonly encounter and must respond to appropriately. Problems may relate to issues delegated to the CEO in Ends and Executive Limitations policies, or they may relate to the board's own job as described in Governance Process and Board-Management Delegation policies. For each scenario, the board member is asked to answer a short series of questions designed to help determine the course of action that should be taken. Governance process and Board-Management Delegation policies, because they fully describe the role of the board and how the role is to be carried out, always guide the appropriate course of action.

The scenarios are presented in four groups. Chapter Three presents scenarios that deal with interactions between the board and its CEO or staff; Chapter Four contains scenarios that deal with individual board member interactions with the CEO or staff; Chapter Five's scenarios are about the governance roles and responsibilities of individual board members; and the scenarios of Chapter Six address the governance job of the board as a team.

Worksheets

Together with the scenario, we provide a worksheet that guides the reader or the board and its members through the steps of a rehearsal. Board members can complete worksheets individually for later comparison, or the board can complete the worksheet as a group. We anticipate that the worksheet will be helpful when the board tackles its "real-life" problems as well. In addition, worksheets can be used by individual board members who are working to enhance their own governance skills. An extra blank worksheet is available in Resource 2.

The Sample Policy Manual

Boards with policy manuals developed according to Policy Governance principles will benefit the most by referring to that document when working through the rehearsals. Boards without such a Policy Governance playbook should use the sample manual in Resource 3, which contains a set of policies that are consistent with the principles of Policy Governance.

Authors' Worksheet Responses

We have formulated responses to all of the scenarios and included those responses in Chapters Three through Six. The purpose of showing our responses is to demonstrate the rehearsal technique. If you are not a board using Policy Governance, reading our responses will help you see how the use of the Policy Governance model enables the board to determine an efficient and effective course of action. We demonstrate that the Board-Management Delegation and Governance Process policies provide guidance to the board when it considers its response to any dilemma. The policies may in some cases contain the entire solution. We hope that our worksheet responses are helpful, but we warn that there may be more than one right answer. Our answers, in other words, are consistent with the policies in the sample manual, but they may not be the only model-consistent answers that are possible.

The Rehearsal Process

The board should describe the problem or issue that it is confronting and then proceed with the following steps.

Step 1

Carefully check the board's policies to identify what has already been said relevant to the issue, writing your findings on your worksheet. Note that more than one policy category is likely to be relevant. For example, the board will have placed its delegation principles in a Board-Management Delegation policy and will have used these principles as it described its expectations of the CEO in Ends and Executive Limitations policies. Write into the appropriate section of the worksheet what you have found in the board's policy manual that is relevant to the rehearsal scenario. The eventual resolution of the scenario, that is, how the board will respond to the situation, will always be a Governance Process or Board-Management Delegation issue (or both).

Step 2

Decide if the scenario refers to any matter that has been delegated to the CEO in Ends and Executive Limitations policies. If your answer is yes, decide if the activity or circumstance of the scenario appears to suggest the accomplishment of a reasonable interpretation of the cited Ends or Executive Limitations policies. If the scenario does not refer to a matter delegated to the CEO, the scenario must be addressing an issue of the board's own job. Decide if the obligations of the board, board members, or committees described in the cited Governance Process and Board-Management Delegation policies have been met.

Step 3

Based on your answers in Step 2, decide the action that the board or board member should take. This action must be consistent with the board's applicable Governance Process and Board-Management Delegation policies. For example, if the scenario deals with a matter of CEO performance and there is reason to believe that a reasonable interpretation of board policy has been accomplished, the board or board member should support the CEO's decision, though the board can change its policies to cause different CEO decisions in the future. Or if the board or board member has failed to act consistently with board expectations, the board must put itself back on track.

Step 4

If you feel that the appropriate response to the scenario is to amend a policy, at this stage you would either suggest an amendment or determine the information that the board would need in order to change the policy.

Step 5

If each board member has been conducting these steps individually, now is the time for the board as a body to discuss and decide the solution to the problem or issue.

Following these rehearsal steps will help the board adhere predictably and reliably to its principles, as well to update and clarify its expectations of itself and its organization.

The worksheet we have included in this book follows these steps. Here is an example of how the worksheet will be completed.

How to Use the Worksheet

Our worksheet will help you rehearse the scenarios we present in the next four chapters. It can be used in a number of ways. The board may wish to collectively complete a worksheet. Or each board member may be asked by the rehearsal leader to individually complete a worksheet prior to full board discussion. Alternatively, individual board members can use the worksheets when they have a question about their role as a member of the board or when deciding on the appropriate way to interact with other people such as staff or owners.

We present each scenario at the top of a worksheet and ask a number of questions to guide you through the steps of the rehearsal. A page showing our response to the scenario follows every scenario worksheet. It may be helpful to compare your answers with ours, though we remind you that although our worksheet responses are consistent with the Policy Governance model and the policies that flow from its principles, there may be other model-consistent responses that better reflect your values. We want you to learn how to solve problems by applying your values in a model-consistent way.

To demonstrate how to fill in the worksheet, consider the following example in which the board rehearsal starts with each board member individually completing a worksheet.

TITLE: Could This Happen to Us?

SCENARIO: A board member of a social service agency hears that a similar agency in another city has been forced to close due to an overwhelming financial loss caused by a successfully prosecuted liability claim. Apparently the agency was underinsured. The board member raises the concern to the board that this could happen to their agency too. What should the board do?

The *first step* is for each board member individually to answer question 1 on the worksheet; "Which board policies are relevant to this scenario?" To answer this question, you must refer either to your own policies or to the manual in Resource 3. We will use Resource 3.

The worksheet asks you to note the policies relevant to this scenario that are found in each policy section of the manual.

Insurance carried by the agency is not an Ends issue, so it is no surprise that there is no reference to this matter in Ends policy. Write "N/A" on your worksheet next to the word *Ends.*

Since the matter of insurance is an operational means issue (delegated to the CEO), you should expect to find policies that are related to it in the Executive Limitations section of the manual. Sure enough, you will find that the board made a broad statement in policy 2.0 prohibiting imprudent conditions (policy numbers refer to the manual in Resource 3). This applies to insurance, as it does to all operational means, but only at a very broad level. Further examination of the Executive Limitations section of the manual reveals that the board has added detail relevant to its prohibition of imprudence in the policy dealing with asset protection, policy 2.6. Initially, the board prohibited actions that result in assets' being unprotected. Further definition of the term *unprotected* is added in policy 2.6.1, where the board states that the CEO shall not "fail to insure against theft and casualty losses to at least 80% replacement value and against liability losses to board members, the staff and the organization itself in an amount greater than the average for comparable organizations." In a related policy (2.6.4), the board prohibited the unnecessary exposure of the organization, its board, or its staff to claims of liability. The board made no further definition of its expectations about insurance.

Write what you have found in Executive Limitations policies on your worksheet, noting the policy numbers and the policy language. A brief summary of the policy language will do if the policy is lengthy.

Next, refer to the policies in the Board-Management Delegation section. These policies are board instructions to the board itself and to its CGO. Here you will find the way the board intends to authorize CEO decision making. Notice that 3.3.2 says that the board will not prescribe but will *proscribe* organizational means. You will find in policy 3.3.3 that any reasonable CEO interpretation of its Ends and Executive Limitations policies will be acceptable. You will also find that the board intends to monitor CEO compliance with Ends and Executive Limitations policies on a schedule that is spelled out in policy 3.4.5. Write these policy numbers and statements on your worksheet.

A check of Governance Process policies (also instructions by the board to itself) turns up no policies about insurance but does reveal policies that address the discipline the board will use to follow through on its intention to delegate decision-making authority to the CEO. It is helpful in your rehearsal to remind yourself that "board members may not attempt to exercise individual authority over the organization" (4.5.3) but that they may "recommend an item for board discussion by submitting the item to the chair no later than 5 days before the board meeting" (4.3.2.C). Note these policy numbers and words on your worksheet.

The *second step* is to answer question 2 on the worksheet, which asks if the scenario refers to anything that the board has delegated to the CEO. Answer yes or no. In this case, the answer will be yes, since the matter is one of operational means. You should go on to question 2a, which asks if the scenario suggests that the CEO has accomplished a reasonable interpretation of the applicable board policies. We are assuming that the board is monitoring its policies and that the required monitoring reports have demonstrated compliance.

The *third step* is to respond to the third worksheet question, which asks what action, if any, the board should take that would be consistent with the board's Governance Process and Board-Management Delegation policies. It would be appropriate to decide that since the board has set out its requirements for insurance and that since these requirements are being met, there is no need to pursue the matter further. But perhaps you are still worried. You may feel that requiring liability insurance "in an amount that is greater than the average for comparable organizations" may be unsatisfactory. You might worry that there are many reasonable indices of comparison, not all of which may be acceptable. It would also be appropriate to exercise your option of recommending to the board that it explore the need for a policy revision, further defining the range of meaning of the word *comparable.*

The *fourth step* is to respond to question 4. This question needs to be answered only if you have suggested that a policy be amended. You may suggest a revision in the policy, but if you are unsure of appropriate language, you may simply identify what information would help you decide if a revision is needed. Write on your worksheet what you need to know. For example, you may wonder if the organization should compare itself with a certain peer group. If so, you would write "Is the appropriate index of comparison one that relates agencies by size, asset base, or client type?"

Your completed worksheet will look like this:

TITLE: Could This Happen to Us?

SCENARIO: A board member of a social service agency hears that a similar agency in another city been forced to close due to an overwhelming financial loss caused by a successfully prosecuted liability claim. Apparently the agency was underinsured. The board member raises the concern to the board that this could happen to their agency too. What should the board do?

Resolve this scenario by answering the following questions:

1. What has the board already said in its relevant policies?

   Ends: *N/A*

   Executive Limitations: *The CEO shall not cause or allow conditions or decisions that are imprudent (2.0). The CEO shall not allow assets to be unprotected (2.6). The CEO shall not fail to insure against theft and casualty losses to at least 80% replacement value and against liability losses to board members, the staff, and the organization itself in an amount greater than the average for comparable organizations (2.6.1). No unnecessary exposure to claims of liability (2.6.4).*

   Board-Management Delegation: *The board will develop policies that limit CEO decision-making latitude regarding means and will never prescribe means (3.3.2). As long as the CEO uses any reasonable interpretation of board policies in Ends and Executive Limitations, the CEO is authorized to make all further decisions (3.3.3). The board will monitor compliance of the asset protection policy annually (3.4.5).*

   Governance Process: *Board members may not attempt to exercise individual authority over the organization (4.5.3). Board members may "recommend an item for board discussion by submitting the item to the chair no later than 5 days before the board meeting" (4.4.2.C).*

2. According to the board's policies, does this scenario refer to anything that has been delegated to the CEO?

   (*circle*)   Yes   No

   Insurance is an operational means matter delegated to the CEO in Executive Limitations policies.

   IF YES:

   2a. Does this scenario suggest that the CEO has accomplished a reasonable interpretation of the board's Ends and Executive Limitations policies?

      (*circle*)   Yes   No   Unsure

      (*Explain your answer.*) *There is no reason to believe that the CEO has violated applicable board policies.*

3. What action, if any, should the board or board member now take? (*Specify the board or board member actions that you believe would be consistent with Governance Process and Board-Management Delegation policies.*) *I suggest that we drop the issue, as it is covered adequately in our existing policies.*

    (*Or you might have written:*) *I suggest that we consider amending the policy about liability insurance, being more specific about what "comparable" means.*

4. If the action you propose involves a possible board policy change:

    4a. What amendments or additions do you suggest? *I suggest that it may be necessary to define "comparable" by specifying if we mean comparable by size, client type, or asset base.*

    4b. What further information, if any, does the board need before deciding on this change? *I suggest that we find out if there are emerging trends in lawsuits brought against organizations of our size, type, or asset base that would distinguish us from other social service organizations. This would help us understand if we should be more restrictive in our policy.*

After board members have completed their worksheets individually, they share their answers with the board as a whole. You will notice that for the most part, board members will have cited the same policies as relevant, although their opinions about policy content and breadth may vary.

After discussion, the board should agree on a course of action representing the board's final disposition of the scenario. Any new policy wording should be recorded in the minutes and for inclusion as an update in the policy manual. If the board decides to collect information before deciding on a policy change, it should indicate what it needs to know, when it needs the information to be available, and who is to see that the information is collected.

The use of the decision-making sequence in the worksheets allows boards to become very familiar with their policies and to grow more disciplined in following their own rules. Further, they become increasingly skilled and confident in using their policies to deal effectively with any situation.

Like most group activities, the rehearsal process may feel awkward or unnatural at first, but it will get easier and take less time as you get more used to it.

Following these rehearsal steps will help the board adhere predictably and reliably to its principles and update and clarify its expectations of itself and its organization.

Hints for Successful Rehearsals

Here are some tips that will help boards make the most of rehearsals. We suggest that you take care to be rigorous about the following items.

1. *Stick to the principles of Policy Governance.* Policy Governance is a system that differs dramatically from traditional governance practice by defining roles and systematic accountability. Because it differs from what is taught by all other governance approaches, it cannot be mixed with non–Policy Governance decision making. No other approach to governance requires the rigorous ends-means distinction of Policy Governance or the architecture of policies arranged by size. No other system enables boards to systematically authorize their delegatees to make any reasonable interpretation of their policies, and no other system requires the rigor that is demanded by Policy Governance when it comes to the use of officers and committees. Looking to other governance approaches to solve issues for a Policy Governance board would be like seeking help from horse riders to enhance car-driving skills. The board must ensure that it thoroughly understands the Policy Governance system, has installed it correctly, and then decides all matters with reference to the principles embodied in the board's own policies.

2. *Stick to the principles of Policy Governance even in a crisis.* We have seen boards that have been confronted with serious crises. Funding cuts and the discovery of fraud are just two examples. While such situations make it tempting to respond too hurriedly to attend to principles, it is the responsibility of the board to act consistent with its governing policies and to ensure that the organization is restored to functioning. This may not involve solving the crisis at the board level but instead seeing to it that the crisis is solved. If the Policy Governance model is of any use to boards, it should surely be useful in bad times as much as or more than in good times. Abandoning the model in times of crisis makes as much sense as a pilot using the flight instruments until there's a storm.

3. *Make appropriate responses to out-of-compliance monitoring reports.* Policy Governance enables boards to be truly accountable for their organizations. It does not make an imperfect world perfect. Accordingly, boards should expect that there will be times when there is organizational noncompliance with their Ends and Executive Limitations policies. When a board receives such information as part of systematic monitoring, it should certainly note the noncompliance. Its response to the noncompliance, however, should be carefully considered. Not every offense should result in the execution of the offender. The board should allow for and consider the pos-

sibility that the policy itself caused the problem—it may have been stated too ambitiously or was impracticable in some other way. If, however, the board is convinced of the appropriateness of the policy, it should consider the option of deciding the time period during which the CEO must correct the problem. There should be further monitoring at the end of that time period. Because we are referring to the CEO's job, under no circumstances should the board take it upon itself to correct the problem: if it were to do so, it would be unable to hold its CEO accountable for righting the situation, and it would further be unable to determine if it had a CEO capable of righting the situation. The board should also not consider changing the policy unless it decided the policy was inappropriate. Changing a policy simply because a CEO cannot or does not comply with it would be like government changing the speeding laws because some drivers don't conform to them.

4. *Be sure to distinguish between monitoring information and incidental information.* Many board members have plenty of opportunity to meet people who are employed by or served by their organization. This causes no problem if it is clear that board members have no authority as individuals to instruct or to judge the organization. Further, it must be clear that monitoring organizational performance must be rigorous and comprehensive. Remember that even several staff member complaints in an organization that employs hundreds of people does not necessarily mean that there is a problem. Unfortunately, it is not uncommon for a board member to hear that a certain staff member or consumer is unhappy about something and to assume that there must be something wrong in the organization. Staff and consumer feedback of the type described is always incidental and an allegation, not a fact. The board member must refer to the policy manual to ascertain if the reported issue, if true, would be a policy violation. The board member has the option of requesting that the board demand an extra monitoring of the policy he or she feels may have been violated.

5. *Remember that if the organization (as opposed to the board itself) is out of compliance with a board policy, the CEO is always accountable for it.* If a board has decided to use Policy Governance and has decided to use a CEO position, then it follows that organizational noncompliance with board Ends and Executive Limitations policies is the accountability of the CEO no matter who under the CEO's authority actually caused the problem. If staff recruitment, curriculum design, or accounting has failed to comply with Executive Limitations policies or if consumer results are not being produced in accordance with Ends policies, the board must hold the CEO accountable for the problem and for fixing the problem, rather than searching in the

organization for the guilty party. Accounting or human resources failed to perform, from the point of view of the board, because the CEO allowed the failure. The Policy Governance board gives the CEO enough authority to ensure that major failures in the face of realistic expectations are unlikely and to hold the CEO accountable for any that occur. External factors not under the control of the CEO may cause out-of-compliance situations too. In such cases, the CEO is still accountable but not blameworthy. These are situations when a board may consider changing its policy so that the CEO has job expectations that he or she has a chance of meeting.

6. *Define policies to as specific a level as the board deems necessary.* Some boards leave their polices at a very broad level, declining to define them further, when in fact they are unwilling to accept the full range of reasonable interpretations of their words. This sets up their delegatee for failure and the system for game playing.

7. *Define policies only to the level of specificity that allows the board to accept any reasonable interpretation.* The Policy Governance board defines its policies to the level of specificity at which it would be satisfied with the accomplishment (Ends) or avoidance of any reasonable interpretation of its words (Executive Limitations). Just because all words can be further defined does not mean that the board should do the defining. To do so would be an attempt by the board to control all it can, rather than all it must.

8. *Move on after a fair and inclusive decision process has reached a conclusion.* All board members should be given the opportunity and time to contribute their points of view. However, when a decision has been made, the dissenting board member or members can hold the process hostage only if the board and its CGO permit this to happen.

9. *Use the consent agenda.* The consent agenda, outlined in Resource 1, is used by Policy Governance boards to assist them in complying with externally imposed requirements.

Part Two
Rehearsal Scenarios

PART TWO PROVIDES an opportunity to practice problem solving using Policy Governance principles. Its four chapters present collections of scenarios for you to resolve. Each chapter deals with one of four types of challenges encountered by boards. Chapter Three deals with interactions between the board and its CEO or staff. Chapter Four covers individual board member interactions with the CEO or staff. Chapter Five concerns the governance roles and responsibilities of individual board members. And Chapter Six addresses the job of the board as a governing team. Each scenario is set forth on a worksheet for you to complete. Following each scenario presented in this way is a worksheet showing our responses to the scenario. You might find it useful to compare your responses to ours.

Rehearsal Scenarios: Board Interactions with the CEO or Staff

IN THIS CHAPTER, we present some scenarios of issues that can arise in the relationship between the board as a body and its CEO, as well as between the board and the CEO's staff. The key issue here is that the scenarios focus on the formal, instructive, and evaluative relationship between the board as a whole (not individual board members) and the operations of the organization. Although this relationship is clearly described in your board's policy manual, or the manual in Resource 3, many boards in practice find that they tend to "make things up as they go along" if a problem or question arises. In this chapter you rehearse using the Policy Governance principles in the policies to solve board-staff issues.

Rehearsal 3.1

TITLE: Is the CEO Planning Ahead?

SCENARIO: The CEO is achieving short-term ends. However, the board is concerned that staff are "flying by the seat of their pants" and do not have formal plans for the achievement of long-term ends. The board wants to be confident that staff are planning ahead but questions whether existing policies address this concern. What should the board do?

Resolve this scenario by answering the following questions:

1. What has the board already said in its relevant policies?

   Ends:

   Executive Limitations:

   Board-Management Delegation:

   Governance Process:

2. According to the board's policies, does this scenario refer to anything that has been delegated to the CEO?

   (circle)   Yes   No

   IF YES:

   2a. Does this scenario suggest that the CEO is in compliance with a reasonable interpretation of the board's Ends and Executive Limitations policies?

   (circle)   Yes   No   Unsure

   (Explain your answer.)

IF NO:

2b. Does this scenario reflect behavior consistent with the board's Governance Process and Board-Management Delegation policies?

(*circle*)   Yes   No   Unsure

(*Explain your answer.*)

3. What action, if any, should the board or board member now take? (*Specify the board or board member actions that you believe would be consistent with Governance Process and Board-Management Delegation policies.*)

4. If the action you propose involves a possible board policy change:

4a. What amendments or additions do you suggest?

4b. What further information, if any, does the board need before deciding on this change?

You are now ready for full board discussion and decision.

Rehearsal 3.1

TITLE: Is the CEO Planning Ahead?

SCENARIO: The CEO is achieving short-term ends. However, the board is concerned that staff are "flying by the seat of their pants" and do not have formal plans for the achievement of long-term ends. The board wants to be confident that staff are planning ahead but questions whether existing policies address this concern. What should the board do?

Resolve this scenario by answering the following questions:

1. What has the board already said in its relevant policies?

   Ends: *N/A*

   Executive Limitations: *The CEO shall not allow material deviation of actual expenditures from board priorities established in Ends policies (2.3), allow budgets that are not derived from a multiyear plan (2.4), or endanger the organization's ability to accomplish ends (2.6.10).*

   Board-Management Delegation: *The board will develop policies that limit the latitude the CEO may exercise in choosing organizational means (3.3.2). As long as the CEO uses any reasonable interpretation of board policies, the CEO can make all further decisions (3.3.3). The board can change its policies (3.3.4).*

   Governance Process: *The board's major policy focus will be on the intended long-term impacts outside the organization, not on the administrative or programmatic means (4.1.2).*

2. According to the board's policies, does this scenario refer to anything that has been delegated to the CEO?

   (*circle*)   (Yes)   No

   The CEO may not fail to have a multiyear plan.

   IF YES:

   2a. Does this scenario suggest that the CEO is in compliance with a reasonable interpretation of the board's Ends and Executive Limitations policies?

   (*circle*)   Yes   No   (Unsure)

   (*Explain your answer.*) *The board is uncertain that the CEO has a long-term plan that is sufficient to allay its concerns. The board's uncertainty may result from inadequate monitoring of policy 2.4 or from inadequate specificity of the policy itself.*

IF NO:

2b. Does this scene reflect behavior consistent with the board's Governance Process and Board-Management Delegation policies?

(*circle*)   Yes   No   Unsure

(*Explain your answer.*)

3. What action, if any, should the board or board member now take? (*Specify the board or board member actions that you believe would be consistent with Governance Process and Board-Management Delegation policies*). *The board should ensure that policy 2.4 has been adequately monitored. If monitoring shows that a reasonable interpretation of the policy has been accomplished, the board may decide that its fears are groundless. If the CEO has reasonably interpreted and complied with the policy but this does not allay the board's concern, the board should consider making its policy more specific.*

4. If the action you propose involves a possible board policy change:

4a. What amendments or additions do you suggest? *The board may increase the specificity of policy 2.4, or it may add a separate Executive Limitations policy addressing the aspects of long-term planning it would find unacceptable.*

4b. What further information, if any, does the board need before deciding on this change? *Board member perspectives of what would constitute inadequate organizational planning.*

You are now ready for full board discussion and decision.

Rehearsal 3.2

TITLE: Should the Board Establish a Committee to Solve a Crisis?

SCENARIO: A trade association loses a significant amount of revenue due to some unforeseen economic conditions. A board member proposes establishing a task force to "work with the staff to develop a business plan for next year." What should the board do?

Resolve this scenario by answering the following questions:

1. What has the board already said in its relevant policies?

   Ends:

   Executive Limitations:

   Board-Management Delegation:

   Governance Process:

2. According to the board's policies, does this scenario refer to anything that has been delegated to the CEO?

   (*circle*)   Yes   No

   IF YES:

   2a. Does this scenario suggest that the CEO is in compliance with a reasonable interpretation of the board's Ends and Executive Limitations policies?

   (*circle*)   Yes   No   Unsure

   (*Explain your answer.*)

IF NO:

2b. Does this scenario reflect behavior consistent with the board's Governance Process and Board-Management Delegation policies?

(*circle*)   Yes   No   Unsure

(*Explain your answer.*)

3. What action, if any, should the board or board member now take? (*Specify the board or board member actions that you believe would be consistent with Governance Process and Board-Management Delegation policies.*)

4. If the action you propose involves a possible board policy change:

4a. What amendments or additions do you suggest?

4b. What further information, if any, does the board need before deciding on this change?

You are now ready for full board discussion and decision.

REHEARSAL WORKSHEET

Rehearsal 3.2

TITLE: Should the Board Establish a Committee to Solve a Crisis?

SCENARIO: A trade association loses a significant amount of revenue due to some unforeseen economic conditions. A board member proposes establishing a task force to "work with the staff to develop a business plan for next year." What should the board do?

Resolve this scenario by answering the following questions:

1. What has the board already said in its relevant policies?

   Ends: *N/A*

   Executive Limitations: *The CEO shall not allow development of fiscal jeopardy or a material deviation of actual expenditures from Ends priorities (2.3); cause or allow financial planning to . . . risk fiscal jeopardy or risk incurring those situations or conditions described as unacceptable in the "Financial Condition and Activities" policy (2.4); fail to report in a timely manner any actual or anticipated noncompliance. (2.8.2); or let the board be unaware of material external changes. (2.8.4.).*

   Board-Management Delegation: *The board will develop policies that limit the latitude the CEO may exercise in choosing the organizational means (3.3.1). The board will never prescribe organizational means (3.3.2). As long as the CEO uses any reasonable interpretation of the board's Ends and Executive Limitations policies, the CEO is authorized to establish all further policies, make all decisions, take all actions, establish all practices, and develop all activities (3.3.3).*

   Governance Process: *The board will enforce upon itself whatever discipline is needed to govern with excellence regarding respect of roles (4.1.3). The board will monitor its performance at each meeting (4.1.6). The CGO's job is to ensure that the board behaves in a manner consistent with its own rules (4.4.1). Board committees are never to interfere with delegation from board to CEO (4.6). Board committees are to help the board do its job, not to help or advise the staff (4.6.1).*

2. According to the board's policies, does this scenario refer to anything that has been delegated to the CEO?

   (*circle*)   Yes   No

   The CEO has been delegated responsibility for financial management, within the parameters set forth in Executive Limitations.

IF YES:

2a. Does this scenario suggest that the CEO is in compliance with a reasonable interpretation of the board's Ends and Executive Limitations policies?

(*circle*)   Yes   No   (Unsure)

(*Explain your answer.*) *The CEO is accountable that organizational performance comply with board policies and, where it does not, that compliance be restored in a timely manner. This scenario does not indicate what the CEO has already done to ensure organizational compliance with board policies.*

IF NO:

2b. Does this scenario reflect behavior consistent with the board's Governance Process and Board-Management Delegation policies?

(*circle*)   Yes   No   Unsure

(*Explain your answer.*)

3. What action, if any, should the board or board member now take? (*Specify the board or board member actions that you believe would be consistent with Governance Process and Board-Management Delegation policies.*) *Board members should notice and bring to the board's attention that setting up the task force would violate its own policies. The board should dismiss the task force idea, as this would interfere with accountable delegation to the CEO. The board should note that the CEO can ask anyone he or she chooses for advise. In light of the unforeseen economic crisis, the board should consider whether it should revisit any of its Ends or Executive Limitations policies.*

4. If the action you propose involves a possible board policy change:

4a. What amendments or additions do you suggest? *A revision of Ends policies, to reflect fewer available resources, may be considered. A revision of the Executive Limitations policy 2.3 prohibiting certain liquidity conditions may also be considered.*

4b. What further information, if any, does the board need before deciding on this change? *The board may find it necessary to collect information about the cost of achieving Ends priorities.*

You are now ready for full board discussion and decision.

Rehearsal 3.3

TITLE: Should the Board Try to Influence Hiring Decisions?

SCENARIO: A past board member applies for an open staff position. During a board meeting, many board members "inform" (with subtle pressure) the CEO "what a great choice he'd be." The CEO conveys that he does not believe that pressure is appropriate and that it is inconsistent with the board's policy regarding respect of roles. What should the board do?

Resolve this scenario by answering the following questions:

1. What has the board already said in its relevant policies?

    Ends:

    Executive Limitations:

    Board-Management Delegation:

    Governance Process:

2. According to the board's policies, does this scenario refer to anything that has been delegated to the CEO?

    (*circle*)   Yes   No

    IF YES:

    2a. Does this scenario suggest that the CEO is in compliance with a reasonable interpretation of the board's Ends and Executive Limitations policies?

    (*circle*)   Yes   No   Unsure

    (*Explain your answer.*)

IF NO:

2b. Does this scenario reflect behavior consistent with the board's Governance Process and Board-Management Delegation policies?

(*circle*)   Yes   No   Unsure

(*Explain your answer.*)

3. What action, if any, should the board or board member now take? (*Specify the board or board member actions that you believe would be consistent with Governance Process and Board-Management Delegation policies.*)

4. If the action you propose involves a possible board policy change:

4a. What amendments or additions do you suggest?

4b. What further information, if any, does the board need before deciding on this change?

You are now ready for full board discussion and decision.

REHEARSAL WORKSHEET

Rehearsal 3.3

TITLE: Should the Board Try to Influence Hiring Decisions?

SCENARIO: A past board member applies for an open staff position. During a board meeting, many board members "inform" (with subtle pressure) the CEO "what a great choice he'd be." The CEO conveys that he does not believe that pressure is appropriate and that it is inconsistent with the board's policy regarding respect of roles. What should the board do?

Resolve this scenario by answering the following questions:

1. What has the board already said in its relevant policies?

   Ends: *N/A*

   Executive Limitations: *The CEO shall not fail to advise the board if the board is not in compliance with its own policies on Governance Process and Board-Management Delegation, particularly in the case of board behavior that is detrimental to the work relationship between the board and the CEO (2.8.5).*

   Board-Management Delegation: *The board will never prescribe organizational means delegated to the CEO (3.3.2).*

   Governance Process: *The board will enforce discipline regarding respect of roles (4.1.3). The CGO ensures that the board behaves consistently with its own rules (4.4.1). Board members will not use their position to obtain employment in the organization for themselves, family members, or close associates (4.5.2.C).*

2. According to the board's policies, does this scenario refer to anything that has been delegated to the CEO?

   (circle)    Yes   No

   Hiring staff is an operational means delegated to the CEO, subject to adherence to Executive Limitations policies. The CEO is also instructed to inform the board if the board doesn't adhere to its own policies.

IF YES:

2a. Does this scenario suggest that the CEO is in compliance with a reasonable interpretation of the board's Ends and Executive Limitations policies?

(*circle*)   (Yes)   No   Unsure

(*Explain your answer.*) *The CEO has recognized that he has responsibility for personnel decisions. He has also met the policy requirement that he notify the board of board actions detrimental to the board-CEO work relationship.*

IF NO:

2b. Does this scenario reflect behavior consistent with the board's Governance Process and Board-Management Delegation policies?

(*circle*)   Yes   No   Unsure

(*Explain your answer.*)

3. What action, if any, should the board or board member now take? (*Specify the board or board member actions that you believe would be consistent with Governance Process and Board-Management Delegation policies.*) *The Board and CGO should recognize that their lobbying actions are interfering in a matter they have authorized the CEO to decide. Board members should notice and bring to the board's attention that it has committed to not prescribing operational means. The board should also remind the CGO of his responsibility to enforce board discipline and discuss how it can be more rigorous in adhering to its own rules.*

4. If the action you propose involves a possible board policy change:

   4a. What amendments or additions do you suggest?

   4b. What further information, if any, does the board need before deciding on this change?

You are now ready for full board discussion and decision.

Rehearsal 3.4

TITLE: Should the Board Select Programs?

SCENARIO: The CEO provides "FYI" or incidental information to the board on the actions she's initiating in order to achieve ends. Board members want to edit, revise, and prioritize these plans. What should the board do?

Resolve this scenario by answering the following questions:

1. What has the board already said in its relevant policies?

   Ends:

   Executive Limitations:

   Board-Management Delegation:

   Governance Process:

2. According to the board's policies, does this scenario refer to anything that has been delegated to the CEO?

   (*circle*)   Yes   No

   IF YES:

   2a. Does this scenario suggest that the CEO is in compliance with a reasonable interpretation of the board's Ends and Executive Limitations policies?

   (*circle*)   Yes   No   Unsure

   (*Explain your answer.*)

IF NO:

2b. Does this scenario reflect behavior consistent with the board's Governance Process and Board-Management Delegation policies?

(*circle*)   Yes   No   Unsure

(*Explain your answer.*)

3. What action, if any, should the board or board member now take? (*Specify the board or board member actions that you believe would be consistent with Governance Process and Board-Management Delegation policies.*)

4. If the action you propose involves a possible board policy change:

4a. What amendments or additions do you suggest?

4b. What further information, if any, does the board need before deciding on this change?

You are now ready for full board discussion and decision.

Rehearsal 3.4

TITLE: Should the Board Select Programs?

SCENARIO: The CEO provides "FYI" or incidental information to the board on the actions she's initiating in order to achieve ends. Board members want to edit, revise, and prioritize these plans. What should the board do?

Resolve this scenario by answering the following questions:

1. What has the board already said in its relevant policies?

   Ends: *N/A*

   Executive Limitations: *The CEO may not let the board be uninformed or unaware of significant incidental information, including material internal and external changes (2.8.4).*

   Board-Management Delegation: *The board will instruct the CEO through Ends and Executive Limitations policies, "allowing the CEO to use any reasonable interpretation of these policies" (3.3). The board will never prescribe organizational means delegated to the CEO (3.3.2). As long as the CEO uses any reasonable interpretation of the board's Ends and Executive Limitations policies, the CEO is authorized to establish all further policies, make all decisions, take all actions, establish all practices, and develop all activities (3.3.3). As long as any particular delegation is in place, the board will respect and support the CEO's choices (3.3.4).*

   Governance Process: *The board's major focus will be on intended impacts, "not on the administrative or programmatic means of attaining those effects" (4.1.2). The board will enforce discipline upon itself, applying to matters such as respect of roles (4.1.3). The board will observe its Governance Process policies scrupulously (4.1.3). The board is responsible for ensuring successful organizational performance on Ends and Executive Limitations (4.2.3). The board may establish other outputs for which it holds itself directly responsible (4.2 notation). The CGO assures the integrity of the board's process (4.4). Meeting discussion content will be on those issues that according to board policy clearly belong to the board to decide (4.4.1.A).*

2. According to the board's policies, does this scenario refer to anything that has been delegated to the CEO?

   (*circle*)   Yes   No

   The board has given the CEO authority to establish activities, subject to the boundaries of Executive Limitations. The CEO also has the obligation to provide certain incidental information to the board.

IF YES:

2a. Does this scenario suggest that the CEO is in compliance with a reasonable interpretation of the board's Ends and Executive Limitations policies?

(*circle*)   (Yes)   No   Unsure

(*Explain your answer.*) *The CEO has recognized that she is responsible for developing the plans to achieve organizational ends and that she may not fail to keep the board informed.*

IF NO:

2b. Does this scenario reflect behavior consistent with the board's Governance Process and Board-Management Delegation policies?

(*circle*)   Yes   No   Unsure

(*Explain your answer.*)

3. What action, if any, should the board or board member now take? (*Specify the board or board member actions that you believe would be consistent with Governance Process and Board-Management Delegation policies.*) *The CGO should remind the board that it has clearly established principles of policymaking and delegation, which are to be upheld. If the board steps in and does the work that has been delegated to the CEO, there will no longer be clear accountability for organizational success or failure.*

   If the desire to revise plans is due to specific concerns, these should be discussed so that the board is confident that its collective concerns about unacceptable means are addressed in board policy. It is imperative that the board judge the CEO's actions in light of board policy, not the individual preferences of board members.

4. If the action you propose involves a possible board policy change:

4a. What amendments or additions do you suggest?

4b. What further information, if any, does the board need before deciding on this change?

You are now ready for full board discussion and decision.

Rehearsal 3.5

TITLE: What If the CEO Lies?

SCENARIO: The board discovers that the organization's finances are out of compliance with board policies. This fact appears to have been deliberately withheld by the CEO. What should the board do?

Resolve this scenario by answering the following questions:

1. What has the board already said in its relevant policies?

    Ends:

    Executive Limitations:

    Board-Management Delegation:

    Governance Process:

2. According to the board's policies, does this scenario refer to anything that has been delegated to the CEO?

    (*circle*)   Yes   No

    IF YES:

    2a. Does this scenario suggest that the CEO is in compliance with a reasonable interpretation of the board's Ends and Executive Limitations policies?

    (*circle*)   Yes   No   Unsure

    (*Explain your answer.*)

IF NO:

2b. Does this scenario reflect behavior consistent with the board's Governance Process and Board-Management Delegation policies?

(*circle*)   Yes   No   Unsure

(*Explain your answer.*)

3. What action, if any, should the board or board member now take? (*Specify the board or board member actions that you believe would be consistent with Governance Process and Board-Management Delegation policies.*)

4. If the action you propose involves a possible board policy change:

4a. What amendments or additions do you suggest?

4b. What further information, if any, does the board need before deciding on this change?

You are now ready for full board discussion and decision.

REHEARSAL WORKSHEET

Rehearsal 3.5

TITLE: What If the CEO Lies?

SCENARIO: The board discovers that the organization's finances are out of compliance with board policies. This fact appears to have been deliberately withheld by the CEO. What should the board do?

Resolve this scenario by answering the following questions:

1. What has the board already said in its relevant policies?

   Ends: *N/A*

   Executive Limitations: *The CEO shall not cause or allow a violation of business or professional ethics (2.0); allow the development of fiscal jeopardy (2.4); endanger the organization's ability to accomplish ends (2.6.10); neglect to submit monitoring data in a timely, accurate, and understandable fashion (2.8.1); or fail to report in a timely manner any actual or anticipated noncompliance with any policy of the board (2.8.2).*

   Board-Management Delegation: *Successful CEO performance is accomplishment of ends and compliance with Executive Limitations (3.2.3). Monitoring of CEO performance will be solely against Ends and Executive Limitations policies (3.4). The board will acquire monitoring data by internal reports, external reports, and direct inspection (3.4.2). The standard for compliance is "any reasonable interpretation" of board policies being monitored. The board is the final arbiter of reasonableness (3.4.3). The board may monitor any policy at any time (3.4.5).*

   Governance Process: *The board's purpose includes ensuring that the organization avoids unacceptable actions and situations (4.0). The board is accountable for successful organizational performance on Ends and Executive Limitations (4.2.3).*

2. According to the board's policies, does this scenario refer to anything that has been delegated to the CEO?

   (*circle*)   Yes   No

   The CEO has responsibility for the management of finances, as well as for ensuring that the board is informed of any aspect of operations not in compliance with its policies.

IF YES:

2a. Does this scenario suggest that the CEO is in compliance with a reasonable interpretation of the board's Ends and Executive Limitations policies?

(*circle*)   Yes   (No)   Unsure

(*Explain your answer.*) *The CEO has failed to comply with two major policy areas: financial condition and board communications. If there has been deliberate withholding of such information, the CEO has also violated the board's policies about ethical performance.*

IF NO:

2b. Does this scenario reflect behavior consistent with the board's Governance Process and Board-Management Delegation policies?

(*circle*)   Yes   No   Unsure

(*Explain your answer.*)

3. What action, if any, should the board or board member now take? (*Specify the board or board member actions that you believe would be consistent with Governance Process and Board-Management Delegation policies.*) *Assuming that a board views its financial expectations as appropriate and doable, it must consider its response to the CEO's noncompliance. Its options range from exercising patience and deciding by when the problem is to be rectified to removing the CEO. If it is determined that the CEO has been dishonest in monitoring, the board's response must be unequivocal, as it cannot exercise its accountability if the veracity of the CEO's communications cannot be relied on. Boards should not exercise patience with CEOs who deceive them.*

4. If the action you propose involves a possible board policy change:

4a. What amendments or additions do you suggest?

4b. What further information, if any, does the board need before deciding on this change?

You are now ready for full board discussion and decision.

Rehearsal 3.6

TITLE: Should the Board Give Its Approval When Asked?

SCENARIO: When providing the board with an "operational update," the CEO asks the board if certain organizational activities are acceptable. How should the board respond?

Resolve this scenario by answering the following questions:

1. What has the board already said in its relevant policies?

   Ends:

   Executive Limitations:

   Board-Management Delegation:

   Governance Process:

2. According to the board's policies, does this scenario refer to anything that has been delegated to the CEO?

   (*circle*)   Yes   No

   IF YES:

   2a. Does this scenario suggest that the CEO is in compliance with a reasonable interpretation of the board's Ends and Executive Limitations policies?

   (*circle*)   Yes   No   Unsure

   (*Explain your answer.*)

IF NO:

2b. Does this scenario reflect behavior consistent with the board's Governance Process and Board-Management Delegation policies?

(*circle*)   Yes   No   Unsure

(*Explain your answer.*)

3. What action, if any, should the board or board member now take? (*Specify the board or board member actions that you believe would be consistent with Governance Process and Board-Management Delegation policies.*)

4. If the action you propose involves a possible board policy change:

4a. What amendments or additions do you suggest?

4b. What further information, if any, does the board need before deciding on this change?

You are now ready for full board discussion and decision.

REHEARSAL WORKSHEET

Rehearsal 3.6

TITLE: Should the Board Give Its Approval When Asked?

SCENARIO: When providing the board with an "operational update," the CEO asks the board if certain organizational activities are acceptable. How should the board respond?

Resolve this scenario by answering the following questions:

1. What has the board already said in its relevant policies?

   Ends: *N/A*

   Executive Limitations: *The CEO shall not let the board be unaware of any significant incidental information including material internal and external changes (2.8.4) or present information to the board without differentiating among monitoring, decision preparation, and other information (2.8.6).*

   Board-Management Delegation: *As long as the CEO uses any reasonable interpretation of the board's Ends and Executive Limitations policies, the CEO is authorized to establish all further policies, make all decisions, and so on (3.3.3).*

   Governance Process: *The CGO's job is to ensure that meeting discussion will focus exclusively on issues that belong to the board to decide or monitor (4.4.1.A). The board will enforce discipline regarding respect of roles (4.1.3).*

2. According to the board's policies, does this scenario refer to anything that has been delegated to the CEO?

   (*circle*)   (Yes)   No

   The CEO is delegated the authority to make operational decisions and to interpret the board's policies as set forth in Ends and Executive Limitations policies.

   IF YES:

2a. Does this scenario suggest that the CEO is in compliance with a reasonable interpretation of the board's Ends and Executive Limitations policies?

   (*circle*)   Yes   (No)   Unsure

   (*Explain your answer.*) *The board has delegated the right to the CEO to make operational decisions, which must be within the parameters established in Ends and Executive Limitations policies. The board has also required that the CEO include her interpretations in monitoring reports giving the board a formal opportunity to judge their "reasonableness."*

Requesting approval of activities through the provision of incidental information is inconsistent with the board's expectations regarding how it is to receive information.

IF NO:

2b. Does this scenario reflect behavior consistent with the board's Governance Process and Board-Management Delegation policies?

(*circle*)   Yes   No   Unsure

(*Explain your answer.*)

3. What action, if any, should the board or board member now take? (*Specify the board or board member actions that you believe would be consistent with Governance Process and Board-Management Delegation policies.*) *Board members should note that the CEO is inviting the board to alter its delegation style by approving operational means. This would harm the board's ability to hold the CEO accountable for delegated performance. The board should remind itself of its commitment to control organizational means by prohibiting those that are unacceptable and not by approving CEO plans. The CGO should ensure that the board adheres to its delegation policies by controlling the agenda and ruling on unnecessary items or actions.*

   The board may also consider whether the CEO does not trust it to accept any reasonable interpretation of its policies and thus feels the need to protect himself or herself by obtaining approvals.

4. If the action you propose involves a possible board policy change:

   4a. What amendments or additions do you suggest? *The board could consider amending the agenda planning policy (4.3) to specify how it will address incidental information on the board agenda.*

   4b. What further information, if any, does the board need before deciding on this change? *The board should discuss if presentation of incidental information should appear at all on its formal agenda. Some boards choose to allow board members to be informed via "operational updates" prior to convening or after adjournment of the board meeting.*

   You are now ready for full board discussion and decision.

Rehearsal 3.7

TITLE: CEO Evaluation and Compensation: Can They Be Done Fairly?

SCENARIO: The board is extremely anxious regarding CEO evaluation and compensation decisions. It wishes to be objective and fair and wonders if it has a system to accomplish this. What should it do?

Resolve this scenario by answering the following questions:

1. What has the board already said in its relevant policies?

   Ends:

   Executive Limitations:

   Board-Management Delegation:

   Governance Process:

2. According to the board's policies, does this scenario refer to anything that has been delegated to the CEO?

   (*circle*)   Yes   No

   IF YES:

   2a. Does this scenario suggest that the CEO is in compliance with a reasonable interpretation of the board's Ends and Executive Limitations policies?

   (*circle*)   Yes   No   Unsure

   (*Explain your answer.*)

IF NO:

2b. Does this scenario reflect behavior consistent with the board's Governance Process and Board-Management Delegation policies?

(*circle*)   Yes   No   Unsure

(*Explain your answer.*)

3. What action, if any, should the board or board member now take? (*Specify the board or board member actions that you believe would be consistent with Governance Process and Board-Management Delegation policies.*)

4. If the action you propose involves a possible board policy change:

4a. What amendments or additions do you suggest?

4b. What further information, if any, does the board need before deciding on this change?

You are now ready for full board discussion and decision.

Rehearsal 3.7

TITLE: CEO Evaluation and Compensation: Can They Be Done Fairly?

SCENARIO: The board is extremely anxious regarding CEO evaluation and compensation decisions. It wishes to be objective and fair and wonders if it has a system to accomplish this. What should it do?

Resolve this scenario by answering the following questions:

1. What has the board already said in its relevant policies?

   Ends: *N/A*

   Executive Limitations: *N/A*

   Board-Management Delegation: *Accomplishment of ends and compliance with Executive Limitations will be viewed as successful CEO performance (3.2.3). Monitoring will be systematic and rigorous against the only expected CEO job outputs: accomplishment of ends and operation within boundaries established in Executive Limitations (3.4). The board will judge both the reasonableness of the interpretation and whether data demonstrate accomplishment of the interpretation (3.4.3). The standard for compliance will be any reasonable CEO interpretation (3.4.4).*

   Governance Process: *Continual board development will include orientation of new board members in the board's Governance Process and periodic board discussion of process improvement (4.1.4). The board must assure that the organization successfully accomplishes ends and avoids unacceptable means (4.2.3). CEO remuneration will be decided after a review of monitoring reports received in the last year during the month of February (4.3.5).*

2. According to the board's policies, does this scenario refer to anything that has been delegated to the CEO?

   (*circle*)   Yes   (No)

   The board is responsible for decisions regarding terms of employment and compensation of the CEO.

   IF YES:

2a. Does this scenario suggest that the CEO is in compliance with a reasonable interpretation of the board's Ends and Executive Limitations policies?

   (*circle*)   Yes   No   Unsure

   (*Explain your answer.*)

IF NO:

2b. Does this scenario reflect behavior consistent with the board's Governance Process and Board-Management Delegation policies?

(*circle*)   Yes   No   (Unsure)

(*Explain your answer.*) *The board appears to be unfamiliar with its own policies, which, if followed, ensure a fair system for CEO evaluation. The policies do not, however, address principles that might be used in determining CEO compensation.*

3. What action, if any, should the board or board member now take? (*Specify the board or board member actions that you believe would be consistent with Governance Process and Board-Management Delegation policies.*) *The board should follow the system outlined in its policies to evaluate CEO performance. The board should also discuss the principles upon which it will decide CEO compensation: its relationship to market, whether it should be performance-based, if it should include a bonus plan, the criteria for such, and so on. The board may choose to enlist the help of a compensation specialist to help reach a decision on this matter.*

4. If the action you propose involves a possible board policy change:

4a. What amendments or additions do you suggest? *The board may want to document the principles it will use to guide decisions on CEO compensation, by creating a new policy on CEO compensation in Board-Management Delegation.*

4b. What further information, if any, does the board need before deciding on this change? *The board may find it valuable to obtain compensation and benefit studies for comparable positions (commonly available from such sources as trade associations and chambers of commerce).*

You are now ready for full board discussion and decision.

Rehearsal 3.8

TITLE: Does the CEO Really Have Decision-Making Authority?

SCENARIO: The organization has a new CEO. In reading the policies, she has several questions concerning Ends and Executive Limitations. She has asked the board to define what it means by the various policies and how it interprets certain vague phrases. What should the board do?

Resolve this scenario by answering the following questions:

1. What has the board already said in its relevant policies?

   Ends:

   Executive Limitations:

   Board-Management Delegation:

   Governance Process:

2. According to the board's policies, does this scenario refer to anything that has been delegated to the CEO?

   (*circle*)   Yes   No

   IF YES:

2a. Does this scenario suggest that the CEO is in compliance with a reasonable interpretation of the board's Ends and Executive Limitations policies?

   (*circle*)   Yes   No   Unsure

   (*Explain your answer.*)

IF NO:

2b. Does this scenario reflect behavior consistent with the board's Governance Process and Board-Management Delegation policies?

(*circle*)   Yes   No   Unsure

(*Explain your answer.*)

3. What action, if any, should the board or board member now take? (*Specify the board or board member actions that you believe would be consistent with Governance Process and Board-Management Delegation policies.*)

4. If the action you propose involves a possible board policy change:

4a. What amendments or additions do you suggest?

4b. What further information, if any, does the board need before deciding on this change?

You are now ready for full board discussion and decision.

Rehearsal 3.8

TITLE: Does the CEO Really Have Decision-Making Authority?

SCENARIO: The organization has a new CEO. In reading the policies, she has several questions concerning Ends and Executive Limitations. She has asked the board to define what it means by the various policies and how it interprets certain vague phrases. What should the board do?

Resolve this scenario by answering the following questions:

1. What has the board already said in its relevant policies?

   Ends: *N/A*

   Executive Limitations: *The CEO shall not neglect to submit monitoring data required by the board in a timely, accurate, and understandable fashion, directly addressing provisions of board policies being monitored (2.8.1).*

   Board-Management Delegation: *The board will instruct the CEO through written Ends and Executive Limitations policies, allowing the CEO to use any reasonable interpretation of these policies (3.3). As long as the CEO uses any reasonable interpretation of the Ends and Executive Limitations policies, "the CEO is authorized to establish all further policies, make all decisions, take all actions, establish all practices, and develop all activities. Such decisions shall have full force and authority as if decided by the board" (3.3.3). The board will judge "the reasonableness of the CEO's interpretation" (3.4.3).*

   Governance Process: *N/A*

2. According to the board's policies, does this scenario refer to anything that has been delegated to the CEO?

   (circle)   Yes   No

   The decision-making authority of the CEO lies in making interpretations of the board's Ends and Executive Limitations policies.

   IF YES:

2a. Does this scenario suggest that the CEO is in compliance with a reasonable interpretation of the board's Ends and Executive Limitations policies?

   (circle)   Yes   No   Unsure

   (Explain your answer.) *The CEO's job is to make decisions that are a reasonable interpretation of the board's Ends and Executive Limitations policies. The CEO is asking the board to do the very work it has delegated to her.*

IF NO:

2b. Does this scenario reflect behavior consistent with the board's Governance Process and Board-Management Delegation policies?

(*circle*)   Yes   (No)   Unsure

(*Explain your answer.*)

3. What action, if any, should the board or board member now take? (*Specify the board or board member actions that you believe would be consistent with Governance Process and Board-Management Delegation policies.*) *The board should affirm to the CEO that she is empowered to use any reasonable interpretation of Ends and Executive Limitations policies, regardless of their degree of specificity. If the policy is vague, it provides the CEO with greater latitude of interpretation. The monitoring process requires and enables the board to judge the reasonableness of the CEO's interpretations.*

4. If the action you propose involves a possible board policy change:

4a. What amendments or additions do you suggest?

4b. What further information, if any, does the board need before deciding on this change?

You are now ready for full board discussion and decision.

Rehearsal 3.9

TITLE: "We've Been Busy!" Is This Ends Monitoring?

SCENARIO: An ends monitoring report discloses CEO interpretations the board considers reasonable, but the data presented are simply an account of the extensive efforts (meetings, programs, and so on) that staff have taken to achieve the ends. What should the board do?

Resolve this scenario by answering the following questions:

1. What has the board already said in its relevant policies?

    Ends:

    Executive Limitations:

    Board-Management Delegation:

    Governance Process:

2. According to the board's policies, does this scenario refer to anything that has been delegated to the CEO?

    (*circle*)   Yes   No

    IF YES:

    2a. Does this scenario suggest that the CEO is in compliance with a reasonable interpretation of the board's Ends and Executive Limitations policies?

    (*circle*)   Yes   No   Unsure

    (*Explain your answer.*)

IF NO:

2b. Does this scenario reflect behavior consistent with the board's Governance Process and Board-Management Delegation policies?

(*circle*)   Yes   No   Unsure

(*Explain your answer.*)

3. What action, if any, should the board or board member now take? (*Specify the board or board member actions that you believe would be consistent with Governance Process and Board-Management Delegation policies.*)

4. If the action you propose involves a possible board policy change:

4a. What amendments or additions do you suggest?

4b. What further information, if any, does the board need before deciding on this change?

You are now ready for full board discussion and decision.

REHEARSAL WORKSHEET

Rehearsal 3.9

TITLE: "We've Been Busy!" Is This Ends Monitoring?

SCENARIO: An ends monitoring report discloses CEO interpretations the board considers reasonable, but the data presented are simply an account of the extensive efforts (meetings, programs, and so on) that staff have taken to achieve the ends. What should the board do?

Resolve this scenario by answering the following questions:

1. What has the board already said in its relevant policies?

   Ends: *N/A*

   Executive Limitations: *The CEO may not neglect to submit monitoring data directly addressing policy criteria (2.8.1).*

   Board-Management Delegation: *Successful CEO performance is organizational accomplishment of Ends and compliance with Executive Limitations (3.2.3). Ends are defined as results, recipients, and cost (3.3.1). Monitoring of CEO job performance is against Ends and Executive Limitations policies only (3.4). The CEO discloses compliance information to the board in internal reports (3.4.2.A). Information that does not help determine the degree to which board policies are being met will not be considered to be monitoring information (3.4.1).*

   Governance Process: *N/A*

2. According to the board's policies, does this scenario refer to anything that has been delegated to the CEO?

   (*circle*)   (Yes)   No

   The CEO is responsible for providing data to enable the board to determine whether a reasonable interpretation of its Ends policies has been achieved.

   IF YES:

2a. Does this scenario suggest that the CEO is in compliance with a reasonable interpretation of the board's Ends and Executive Limitations policies?

   (*circle*)   Yes   (No)   Unsure

   (*Explain your answer.*) *The CEO has not fulfilled the requirement to submit data substantiating policy compliance (achievement of a reasonable interpretation of the Ends policies).*

IF NO:

2b. Does this scenario reflect behavior consistent with the board's Governance Process and Board-Management Delegation policies?

(*circle*)   Yes   No   Unsure

(*Explain your answer.*)

3. What action, if any, should the board or board member now take? (*Specify the board or board member actions that you believe would be consistent with Governance Process and Board-Management Delegation policies.*) *The CGO should ensure that the board questions whether the CEO's monitoring report discloses both the CEO's interpretation and data that demonstrates accomplishment of the interpretation. In this case, the board would determine that the monitoring report is incomplete and therefore not acceptable. It should decide on a time frame within which the CEO is to fulfill his or her monitoring obligation (2.8.1).*

4. If the action you propose involves a possible board policy change:

4a. What amendments or additions do you suggest?

4b. What further information, if any, does the board need before deciding on this change?

You are now ready for full board discussion and decision.

Rehearsal 3.10

TITLE: We Like and Trust Our CEO: Isn't That Governance?

SCENARIO: A board hired a CEO who was formerly the board chair and is a close personal friend of many board members. CEO actions that appear noncompliant with policy are rarely questioned, and when some board members raise concerns, the majority response is that "we trust her." What should the concerned board members do?

Resolve this scenario by answering the following questions:

1. What has the board already said in its relevant policies?

   Ends:

   Executive Limitations:

   Board-Management Delegation:

   Governance Process:

2. According to the board's policies, does this scenario refer to anything that has been delegated to the CEO?

   (*circle*)   Yes   No

   IF YES:

2a. Does this scenario suggest that the CEO is in compliance with a reasonable interpretation of the board's Ends and Executive Limitations policies?

   (*circle*)   Yes   No   Unsure

   (*Explain your answer.*)

IF NO:

2b. Does this scenario reflect behavior consistent with the board's Governance Process and Board-Management Delegation policies?

(*circle*)   Yes   No   Unsure

(*Explain your answer.*)

3. What action, if any, should the board or board member now take? (*Specify the board or board member actions that you believe would be consistent with Governance Process and Board-Management Delegation policies.*)

4. If the action you propose involves a possible board policy change:

4a. What amendments or additions do you suggest?

4b. What further information, if any, does the board need before deciding on this change?

You are now ready for full board discussion and decision.

Rehearsal 3.10

TITLE: We Like and Trust Our CEO: Isn't That Governance?

SCENARIO: A board hired a CEO who was formerly the board chair and is a close personal friend of many board members. CEO actions that appear noncompliant with policy are rarely questioned, and when some board members raise concerns, the majority response is that "we trust her." What should the concerned board members do?

Resolve this scenario by answering the following questions:

1. What has the board already said in its relevant policies?

   Ends: *N/A*

   Executive Limitations: *N/A*

   Board-Management Delegation: *The board's sole official connection to operations is the CEO (3.0). The board will view CEO performance as identical to organizational performance (3.2.3). Systematic and rigorous monitoring of CEO performance will be solely against Ends and Executive Limitations policies (3.4).*

   Governance Process: *The purpose of the board is to act on behalf of owners to assure appropriate organizational performance (4.0). The board will enforce upon itself whatever discipline is needed to govern with excellence, applying to matters such as respect of roles (4.1.3). The CGO assures the integrity of the board's process (4.4.1). Board members must be loyal to the ownership, unconflicted by loyalties to staff (4.5.1).*

2. According to the board's policies, does this scenario refer to anything that has been delegated to the CEO?

   (*circle*)   Yes   (No)

   The board is responsible for assuring that CEO performance meets policy requirements.

   IF YES:

2a. Does this scenario suggest that the CEO is in compliance with a reasonable interpretation of the board's Ends and Executive Limitations policies?

   (*circle*)   Yes   No   Unsure

   (*Explain your answer.*)

IF NO:

2b. Does this scenario reflect behavior consistent with the board's Governance Process and Board-Management Delegation policies?

(*circle*)   Yes   (No)   Unsure

(*Explain your answer.*) *The board's obligation to the ownership requires that it not just "trust the CEO" but verify that the trust is merited by monitoring her performance against stated policy criteria.*

3. What action, if any, should the board or board member now take? (*Specify the board or board member actions that you believe would be consistent with Governance Process and Board-Management Delegation policies.*) *The board should recognize that although the person they hired may be a friend or peer in a personal context, the CEO works for the board. This separation of roles, and respect of such, is necessary for accountability. Concerned board members should raise the issue, either first with the CGO (who, if aware of this situation, should already have taken steps to reinforce board discipline and rigor) or with the board as a whole. The board should affirm its commitment to owners by clarifying that while it may have implicit trust due to the personal relationships, effective governance requires that the basis for the trust—policy compliance—be rigorously verified through the board's monitoring system.*

4. If the action you propose involves a possible board policy change:

4a. What amendments or additions do you suggest?

4b. What further information, if any, does the board need before deciding on this change?

You are now ready for full board discussion and decision.

Rehearsal 3.11

TITLE: Who's Accountable?

SCENARIO: The board overseeing a major community celebration is extremely upset with staff for allowing too many politicians in the parade. Staff had allowed some in, but the board's parade committee invited or allowed others to participate. How should the board resolve this?

Resolve this scenario by answering the following questions:

1. What has the board already said in its relevant policies?

   Ends:

   Executive Limitations:

   Board-Management Delegation:

   Governance Process:

2. According to the board's policies, does this scenario refer to anything that has been delegated to the CEO?

   (*circle*)   Yes   No

   IF YES:

   2a. Does this scenario suggest that the CEO is in compliance with a reasonable interpretation of the board's Ends and Executive Limitations policies?

   (*circle*)   Yes   No   Unsure

   (*Explain your answer.*)

IF NO:

2b. Does this scenario reflect behavior consistent with the board's Governance Process and Board-Management Delegation policies?

(*circle*)   Yes   No   Unsure

(*Explain your answer.*)

3. What action, if any, should the board or board member now take? (*Specify the board or board member actions that you believe would be consistent with Governance Process and Board-Management Delegation policies.*)

4. If the action you propose involves a possible board policy change:

4a. What amendments or additions do you suggest?

4b. What further information, if any, does the board need before deciding on this change?

You are now ready for full board discussion and decision.

REHEARSAL WORKSHEET

Rehearsal 3.11

TITLE: Who's Accountable?

SCENARIO: The board overseeing a major community celebration is extremely upset with staff for allowing too many politicians in the parade. Staff had allowed some in, but the board's parade committee invited or allowed others to participate. How should the board resolve this?

Resolve this scenario by answering the following questions:

1. What has the board already said in its relevant policies?

   Ends: *N/A*

   Executive Limitations: *The CEO shall not cause or allow any decision, activity, or circumstance that is imprudent (2.0) or endanger the organization's public image (2.6.10).*

   Board-Management Delegation: *Only officially passed motions of the board are binding on the CEO (3.1). Decisions or instructions of committees are not binding on the CEO unless the board has specifically authorized such exercise of authority (3.1.1). The board will never prescribe organizational means (3.3.2). As long as the CEO uses any reasonable interpretation of board Ends and Executive Limitations policies, he or she can make all further decisions (3.3.3).*

   Governance Process: *The board will enforce upon itself whatever discipline is required to govern with excellence, including respect of roles (4.1.3). The board will monitor and discuss its process and performance, comparing board activity and discipline to the policies in Governance Process and Board-Management Delegation categories (4.1.6). The CGO's job includes ensuring that the board behave consistently with its own rules (4.4.1). The board may establish other outputs for which it holds itself directly responsible (4.2 notation). Board committees will never interfere with the delegation from board to CEO (4.6). Expectations and authority of board committees will be carefully stated in order not to conflict with the authority given to the CEO (4.6.2).*

2. According to the board's policies, does this scenario refer to anything that has been delegated to the CEO?

   (*circle*)   (Yes)   No

   Determination of who participates in a program is a means issue, which is delegated to staff. The board's Executive Limitations policies have not withheld authority in this area.

IF YES:

2a. Does this scenario suggest that the CEO is in compliance with a reasonable interpretation of the board's Ends and Executive Limitations policies?

(*circle*) (Yes) No Unsure

(*Explain your answer.*) *The CEO, by inviting politicians into the parade, made a decision that was within his or her authority.*

IF NO:

2b. Does this scenario reflect behavior consistent with the board's Governance Process and Board-Management Delegation policies?

(*circle*) Yes No Unsure

(*Explain your answer.*)

3. What action, if any, should the board or board member now take? (*Specify the board or board member actions that you believe would be consistent with Governance Process and Board-Management Delegation policies.*) *The board is obligated to support CEO decisions that are a reasonable interpretation of board policies.*

   Every board member should notice that having a committee involved in matters already delegated to the CEO violates board policies and makes it impossible for the board to hold either the committee or the CEO accountable for acceptable performance. Options include disbanding the committee or charging it with finding policy alternatives for board consideration regarding participation of politicians. Another option would be for the board to take total responsibility for decisions regarding participation of politicians, but then it could no longer hold the CEO accountable for this aspect of parade content.

   The board should also remind the CGO of the expectation it has that he or she will assure that the board complies with its own policies.

4. If the action you propose involves a possible board policy change:

   4a. What amendments or additions do you suggest? *If the board does not intend to delegate decisions about politician involvement to the CEO, it should make the appropriate amendment to Executive Limitations policy and add these decisions to its own job description.*

   4b. What further information, if any, does the board need before deciding on this change?

   You are now ready for full board discussion and decision.

Rehearsal 3.12

TITLE: Who Makes the Unpopular Choices?

SCENARIO: A school board is aware that the CEO is about to reduce the number of kindergarten hours that will be offered. It knows that some parents will be unhappy with this decision. What should the board do?

Resolve this scenario by answering the following questions:

1. What has the board already said in its relevant policies?

   Ends:

   Executive Limitations:

   Board-Management Delegation:

   Governance Process:

2. According to the board's policies, does this scenario refer to anything that has been delegated to the CEO?

   (*circle*)   Yes   No

   IF YES:

   2a. Does this scenario suggest that the CEO is in compliance with a reasonable interpretation of the board's Ends and Executive Limitations policies?

   (*circle*)   Yes   No   Unsure

   (*Explain your answer.*)

IF NO:

2b. Does this scenario reflect behavior consistent with the board's Governance Process and Board-Management Delegation policies?

(*circle*)   Yes   No   Unsure

(*Explain your answer.*)

3. What action, if any, should the board or board member now take? (*Specify the board or board member actions that you believe would be consistent with Governance Process and Board-Management Delegation policies.*)

4. If the action you propose involves a possible board policy change:

4a. What amendments or additions do you suggest?

4b. What further information, if any, does the board need before deciding on this change?

You are now ready for full board discussion and decision.

Rehearsal 3.12

TITLE: Who Makes the Unpopular Choices?

SCENARIO: A school board is aware that the CEO is about to reduce the number of kindergarten hours that will be offered. It knows that some parents will be unhappy with this decision. What should the board do?

Resolve this scenario by answering the following questions:

1. What has the board already said in its relevant policies?

   Ends: *"Young people will have all the knowledge and ability that will prepare them for the next stage of their lives that can be obtained at a reasonable tax rate" (1.0, example C). "Students entering grade one will be ready to learn" (1.2.A.4, example C).*

   Executive Limitations: *The CEO will not allow a material deviation of expenditures from the board's Ends priorities (2.4) or let the board be unaware of material internal and external changes (2.8.4).*

   Board-Management Delegation: *Accomplishment of Ends and compliance with Executive Limitations will be viewed as successful CEO performance (3.2.3). The board directs the CEO to achieve specific results, for specified recipients, at a specified cost (3.3.1). Executive Limitations limit the latitude the CEO may exercise in choosing organizational means (3.3.2). As long as the CEO uses any reasonable interpretation of these policies, the CEO may make further decisions, which have full force and authority as if decided by the board (3.3.3). As long as any particular delegation is in place, the board will respect and support the CEO's choices (3.3.4).*

   Governance Process: *The board will govern with clear distinction of board and chief executive roles (4.1). As an informed agent of the ownership, the board has responsibility to create the link between the ownership and the operational organization (4.2.1) and written governing policies that address the broadest levels of all organizational decisions, specifically including Ends and Executive Limitations (4.2.2).*

2. According to the board's policies, does this scenario refer to anything that has been delegated to the CEO?

   (*circle*) (Yes) No

   The CEO has responsibility for making operational decisions that will produce achievement of ends and in a manner that avoids unacceptable means.

IF YES:

2a. Does this scenario suggest that the CEO is in compliance with a reasonable interpretation of the board's Ends and Executive Limitations policies?

(*circle*)   (Yes)   No   Unsure

(*Explain your answer.*) *Although the CEO's decision will be unpopular with some people, it is consistent with the latitude of authority set forth in the board's policies. The CEO has fulfilled the policy requirement of informing the board.*

IF NO:

2b. Does this scenario reflect behavior consistent with the board's Governance Process and Board-Management Delegation policies?

(*circle*)   Yes   No   Unsure

(*Explain your answer.*)

3. What action, if any, should the board or board member now take? (*Specify the board or board member actions that you believe would be consistent with Governance Process and Board-Management Delegation policies.*) *Board members should recognize that the CEO, while required to advise the board of material changes, is empowered to make decisions about programs used to achieve ends. The board is obligated to protect the CEO from criticism regarding decisions that are consistent with the board's policies, no matter how unpopular the decisions may be. Recognizing that this decision may cause a public outcry, the board may wish to verify that its policies reflect the needs and wants of the ownership. If the policies are subsequently revised, the CEO will be expected to comply with policy changes.*

4. If the action you propose involves a possible board policy change:

4a. What amendments or additions do you suggest? *If the board is not willing to risk a public outcry, it may add an Executive Limitations policy stating that the CEO may not fail to provide a minimum of so many daily hours of instruction or "extended day" hours for kindergarten students. Assuming that existing ends would still be achieved after the planned change of kindergarten hours, the board should understand that such additional policy will elevate the cost of results to more than is necessary, thus leaving fewer resources for the achievement of other ends.*

4b. What further information, if any, does the board need before deciding on this change?

You are now ready for full board discussion and decision.

Rehearsal 3.13

TITLE: Monitoring Reports? What Monitoring Reports?

SCENARIO: The board has received no monitoring reports from the CEO. What should it do?

Resolve this scenario by answering the following questions:

1. What has the board already said in its relevant policies?

   Ends:

   Executive Limitations:

   Board-Management Delegation:

   Governance Process:

2. According to the board's policies, does this scenario refer to anything that has been delegated to the CEO?

   (*circle*)   Yes   No

   IF YES:

2a. Does this scenario suggest that the CEO is in compliance with a reasonable interpretation of the board's Ends and Executive Limitations policies?

   (*circle*)   Yes   No   Unsure

   (*Explain your answer.*)

IF NO:

2b. Does this scenario reflect behavior consistent with the board's Governance Process and Board-Management Delegation policies?

(*circle*)   Yes   No   Unsure

(*Explain your answer.*)

3. What action, if any, should the board or board member now take? (*Specify the board or board member actions that you believe would be consistent with Governance Process and Board-Management Delegation policies.*)

4. If the action you propose involves a possible board policy change:

4a. What amendments or additions do you suggest?

4b. What further information, if any, does the board need before deciding on this change?

You are now ready for full board discussion and decision.

Rehearsal 3.13

TITLE: Monitoring Reports? What Monitoring Reports?

SCENARIO: The board has received no monitoring reports from the CEO. What should it do?

Resolve this scenario by answering the following questions:

1. What has the board already said in its relevant policies?

   Ends: *N/A*

   Executive Limitations: *The CEO shall not neglect to submit monitoring data required by the board on a timely basis (see policy on monitoring CEO performance) (2.8.1).*

   Board-Management Delegation: *All board policies that instruct the CEO will be monitored at a frequency and by a method chosen by the board. The board will ordinarily depend on a routine schedule, established in policy 3.4.5.*

   Governance Process: *The board's job is to ensure successful organizational performance on Ends and Executive Limitations (4.2.3). The authority of the CGO consists in making decisions that fall within topics covered by board policies on Governance Process and Board-Management Delegation. The CGO is authorized to use any reasonable interpretation of these policies (4.4.2).*

2. According to the board's policies, does this scenario refer to anything that has been delegated to the CEO?

   (circle)   (Yes)   No

   The CEO's delegated responsibilities include providing timely monitoring data to the board.

   IF YES:

   2a. Does this scenario suggest that the CEO is in compliance with a reasonable interpretation of the board's Ends and Executive Limitations policies?

   (circle)   Yes   (No)   Unsure

   (Explain your answer.) *The CEO's obligation to provide monitoring reports to the board has not been fulfilled.*

IF NO:

2b. Does this scenario reflect behavior consistent with the board's Governance Process and Board-Management Delegation policies?

(*circle*)   Yes   No   Unsure

(*Explain your answer.*)

3. What action, if any, should the board or board member now take? (*Specify the board or board member actions that you believe would be consistent with Governance Process and Board-Management Delegation policies.*) *The board must address the failure of the CEO to comply with Executive Limitations policy 2.8.1. The board and particularly the CGO should note that despite its policy commitment to do so, it has failed to monitor performance. A board that does not receive and review monitoring reports cannot fulfill its own accountability for organizational performance. If the situation persists, the board should attend to its own discipline and its expectations of its CGO.*

4. If the action you propose involves a possible board policy change:

4a. What amendments or additions do you suggest?

4b. What further information, if any, does the board need before deciding on this change?

You are now ready for full board discussion and decision.

Rehearsal 3.14

TITLE: If Consumers Are Upset, Does This Mean the CEO Is Wrong?

SCENARIO: The CEO has made a major change to the organization's programming, to the consternation of some consumers. Consumers question how the board could have allowed the CEO to make that decision. What should the board do?

Resolve this scenario by answering the following questions:

1. What has the board already said in its relevant policies?

   Ends:

   Executive Limitations:

   Board-Management Delegation:

   Governance Process:

2. According to the board's policies, does this scenario refer to anything that has been delegated to the CEO?

   (*circle*)   Yes   No

   IF YES:

   2a. Does this scenario suggest that the CEO is in compliance with a reasonable interpretation of the board's Ends and Executive Limitations policies?

   (*circle*)   Yes   No   Unsure

   (*Explain your answer.*)

IF NO:

2b. Does this scenario reflect behavior consistent with the board's Governance Process and Board-Management Delegation policies?

(*circle*)   Yes   No   Unsure

(*Explain your answer.*)

3. What action, if any, should the board or board member now take? (*Specify the board or board member actions that you believe would be consistent with Governance Process and Board-Management Delegation policies.*)

4. If the action you propose involves a possible board policy change:

4a. What amendments or additions do you suggest?

4b. What further information, if any, does the board need before deciding on this change?

You are now ready for full board discussion and decision.

Rehearsal 3.14

TITLE: If Consumers Are Upset, Does This Mean the CEO Is Wrong?

SCENARIO: The CEO has made a major change to the organization's programming, to the consternation of some consumers. Consumers question how the board could have allowed the CEO to make that decision. What should the board do?

Resolve this scenario by answering the following questions:

1. What has the board already said in its relevant policies?

    Ends: *All*

    Executive Limitations: *CEO may not cause or allow any decision that is imprudent (2.0), any material deviation of expenditures from Ends priorities (2.4), or the board to be uninformed of material internal and external changes (2.8.4).*

    Board-Management Delegation: *Organizational accomplishment of ends and avoidance of proscribed means will be viewed as successful CEO performance (3.2). If using a reasonable interpretation of Ends and Executive Limitations policies, the CEO is authorized to establish all practices and develop all activities. Such decisions shall have full force and authority as if decided by the board (3.3.3). As long as any particular delegation is in place, the board will respect and support the CEO's choices (3.3.4).*

    Governance Process: *The board assures achievement of ends and avoidance of unacceptable actions and situations (4.0). Discipline will apply to matters such as respect of roles (4.1.3). The board establishes policies on Executive Limitations (constraints on executive authority) and Ends (products, impacts, benefits, outcomes, recipients, and so on). The board assures successful organizational performance on Ends and Executive Limitations (4.2.3).*

2. According to the board's policies, does this scenario refer to anything that has been delegated to the CEO?

    (*circle*)   No

    The CEO is delegated authority to make programmatic decisions and is also responsible for ensuring that the board is informed of material changes.

IF YES:

2a. Does this scenario suggest that the CEO is in compliance with a reasonable interpretation of the board's Ends and Executive Limitations policies?

(circle)   Yes   No   (Unsure)

(*Explain your answer.*) *The CEO is delegated authority to decide what programs or practices will be used or changed to accomplish ends. If the CEO has violated no Executive Limitations policies and can demonstrate that the change is aimed at the accomplishment of board-stated ends, the CEO is in compliance. The board's monitoring will answer these questions.*

IF NO:

2b. Does this scenario reflect behavior consistent with the board's Governance Process and Board-Management Delegation policies?

(*circle*)   Yes   No   Unsure

(*Explain your answer.*)

3. What action, if any, should the board or board member now take? (*Specify the board or board member actions that you believe would be consistent with Governance Process and Board-Management Delegation policies.*) *If the board determines that the CEO's decision is consistent with its delegated authority, it is obligated to protect the CEO from public criticism. If the CEO's actions were not a reasonable interpretation of board policy, the board should demand rectification of the issue. (Adherence to the policy requiring that the board be informed of material internal and external changes would have ensured that implementation of the CEO's decision did not come as a surprise to the board.)*

4. If the action you propose involves a possible board policy change:

   4a. What amendments or additions do you suggest? *The consumers' consternation is likely with Ends policies that specify or prioritize results for certain populations and not to others. If the CEO's actions were a reasonable interpretation of the current policies but the board is still concerned, reconsideration of Ends policies is indicated.*

   4b. What further information, if any, does the board need before deciding on this change? The board should study options and implications regarding which populations are to benefit.

You are now ready for full board discussion and decision.

REHEARSAL WORKSHEET

Rehearsal 3.15

TITLE: High Expectations, Low Funding: Is There a Solution?

SCENARIO: A tax-funded governmental organization has historically been successful in producing ends. Demand and use have risen, but funding has not increased accordingly. Staff fear that without additional funding, facilities and programs will deteriorate, diminishing the organization's ability to accomplish ends in the future. The CEO has brought this to the attention of the board. The board is afraid that the public won't support a tax increase, even though there hasn't been one for more than a decade. What should the board do?

Resolve this scenario by answering the following questions:

1. What has the board already said in its relevant policies?

    Ends:

    Executive Limitations:

    Board-Management Delegation:

    Governance Process:

2. According to the board's policies, does this scenario refer to anything that has been delegated to the CEO?

    (*circle*)   Yes   No

    IF YES:

    2a. Does this scenario suggest that the CEO is in compliance with a reasonable interpretation of the board's Ends and Executive Limitations policies?

    (circle)   Yes   No   Unsure

    (*Explain your answer.*)

IF NO:

2b. Does this scenario reflect behavior consistent with the board's Governance Process and Board-Management Delegation policies?

(circle)   Yes   No   Unsure

(Explain your answer.)

3. What action, if any, should the board or board member now take? (*Specify the board or board member actions that you believe would be consistent with Governance Process and Board-Management Delegation policies.*)

4. If the action you propose involves a possible board policy change:

4a. What amendments or additions do you suggest?

4b. What further information, if any, does the board need before deciding on this change?

You are now ready for full board discussion and decision.

Rehearsal 3.15

TITLE: High Expectations, Low Funding: Is There a Solution?

SCENARIO: A tax-funded governmental organization has historically been successful in producing ends. Demand and use have risen, but funding has not increased accordingly. Staff fear that without additional funding, facilities and programs will deteriorate, diminishing the organization's ability to accomplish ends in the future. The CEO has brought this to the attention of the board. The board is afraid that the public won't support a tax increase, even though there hasn't been one for more than a decade. What should the board do?

Resolve this scenario by answering the following questions:

1. What has the board already said in its relevant policies?

   Ends: *Ends will be achieved for the public with available funds (1.0, example C).*

   Executive Limitations: *The CEO will not allow any decision or circumstance that is imprudent (2.0); fail to have financial planning derived from a multiyear plan (2.4); allow assets to be unprotected, inadequately maintained, or unnecessarily risked (2.6); endanger the organization's ability to achieve ends (2.6.10); allow the board to be uninformed or unsupported in its work (2.8); fail to report any anticipated noncompliance with any policy of the board (2.8.2); let the board be unaware of relevant trends (2.8.3); or fail to advise the board if the board is not in compliance with its own policies, particularly in the case of board behavior detrimental to the work relationship between the board and the CEO (2.8.5).*

   Board-Management Delegation: *The board holds the CEO accountable for a reasonable interpretation of its Ends and Executive Limitations policies (3.4.3).*

   Governance Process: *The board acts on behalf of the ownership to see to it that results are achieved at an "appropriate" cost (4.0). The board will govern with an emphasis on the future and on proactivity (4.1). As an informed agent of the ownership, the board will produce the link between the organization and the ownership (4.2.1), establish realistic Ends policies (4.2.2), and assure successful performance on Ends and Executive Limitations (4.2.3). Agendas may include the board's being educated by staff regarding Ends determinations (4.3.2.B). The CGO is to see to it that the board behaves consistently with its own rules (4.4.1.A). The board must be loyal to the ownership and avoid conflicts of interest with respect to its fiduciary responsibility (4.5.1).*

2. According to the board's policies, does this scenario refer to anything that has been delegated to the CEO?

   (*circle*)   (Yes)   No

   The CEO is delegated responsibility for achievement of ends, within limits described in Executive Limitations policies, and for notifying the board of an anticipated noncompliance with the board's Ends or Executive Limitations.

   IF YES:

   2a. Does this scenario suggest that the CEO is in compliance with a reasonable interpretation of the board's Ends and Executive Limitations policies?

       (*circle*)   (Yes)   No   Unsure

       (*Explain your answer.*) *The CEO has complied with his obligation to inform the board of material changes and of anticipated inability to comply with Ends and Executive Limitations policies.*

   IF NO:

   2b. Does this scenario reflect behavior consistent with the board's Governance Process and Board-Management Delegation policies?

       (*circle*)   Yes   No   Unsure

       (*Explain your answer.*)

3. What action, if any, should the board or board member now take? (*Specify the board or board member actions that you believe would be consistent with Governance Process and Board-Management Delegation policies.*) *The board has an obligation to weigh the CEO's input when deliberating its Ends policies. As the agent of the ownership, it must consider the need to raise taxes or reduce the expectations it has of its organization. The board may need to enhance its communications with owners so that they have a realistic grasp of what results can be attained for what costs.*

4. If the action you propose involves a possible board policy change:

   4a. What amendments or additions do you suggest? *The board's intended communications with owners should be expressed in an amendment to the Governance Process policy on agenda planning or as a new policy on ownership linkage. As a result of these consultations, the board may amend Ends policies.*

   4b. What further information, if any, does the board need before deciding on this change?

   You are now ready for full board discussion and decision.

Rehearsal 3.16

TITLE: "Unrealistic Ends"? Says Who?

SCENARIO: The Arts Council board has established Ends policies requiring results that the CEO believes are unattainable given available resources. The CEO has told the board of his opinion. What should the board do?

Resolve this scenario by answering the following questions:

1. What has the board already said in its relevant policies?

    Ends:

    Executive Limitations:

    Board-Management Delegation:

    Governance Process:

2. According to the board's policies, does this scenario refer to anything that has been delegated to the CEO?

    (*circle*)   Yes   No

    IF YES:

    2a. Does this scenario suggest that the CEO is in compliance with a reasonable interpretation of the board's Ends and Executive Limitations policies?

    (*circle*)   Yes   No   Unsure

    (*Explain your answer.*)

IF NO:

2b. Does this scenario reflect behavior consistent with the board's Governance Process and Board-Management Delegation policies?

(*circle*)   Yes   No   Unsure

(*Explain your answer.*)

3. What action, if any, should the board or board member now take? (*Specify the board or board member actions that you believe would be consistent with Governance Process and Board-Management Delegation policies.*)

4. If the action you propose involves a possible board policy change:

4a. What amendments or additions do you suggest?

4b. What further information, if any, does the board need before deciding on this change?

You are now ready for full board discussion and decision.

REHEARSAL WORKSHEET

Rehearsal 3.16

TITLE: "Unrealistic Ends"? Says Who?

SCENARIO: The Arts Council board has established Ends policies requiring results that the CEO believes are unattainable given available resources. The CEO has told the board of his opinion. What should the board do?

Resolve this scenario by answering the following questions:

1. What has the board already said in its relevant policies?

   Ends: *Policy 1.0, example F*

   Executive Limitations: *CEO may not allow the board to be uninformed (2.8); fail to report an anticipated noncompliance with any policy of the board (2.8.2); or fail to advise the board if the board is not in compliance with its own policies, particularly if detrimental to the work relationship between the board and the CEO (2.8.5).*

   Board-Management Delegation: *Decisions of the board are binding on the CEO (3.1). Successful CEO performance requires accomplishment of board-stated ends (3.2.3). The board will develop Ends policies instructing the CEO to achieve specified results for specified recipients at a specified cost (3.3.1). The board will monitor CEO performance against a reasonable interpretation of its Ends and Executive Limitations policies (3.4). There is annual internal monitoring reporting on all Ends policies (3.4.5).*

   Governance Process: *The board's purpose is to ensure achievement of results for an appropriate cost (4.0). The board is responsible to create realistic written governing policies (4.2.2) and for assurance of successful organizational performance on Ends and Executive Limitations (4.2.3). Staff input will be used to inform the board's ends deliberations (4.3.2.B). CEO monitoring will be on the agenda if policy criteria are to be debated (4.3.4).*

2. According to the board's policies, does this scenario refer to anything that has been delegated to the CEO?

   (*circle*)   (Yes)   No

   The CEO is delegated responsibility for accomplishing ends and avoiding unacceptable means.

IF YES:

2a. Does this scenario suggest that the CEO is in compliance with a reasonable interpretation of the board's Ends and Executive Limitations policies?

(*circle*)   (Yes)   No   Unsure

(*Explain your answer.*) *The CEO has fulfilled his obligation to notify the board of the anticipated failure to achieve ends and of his belief that the Ends policies are not realistic.*

IF NO:

2b. Does this scenario reflect behavior consistent with the board's Governance Process and Board-Management Delegation policies?

(*circle*)   Yes   No   Unsure

(*Explain your answer.*)

3. What action, if any, should the board or board member now take? (*Specify the board or board member actions that you believe would be consistent with Governance Process and Board-Management Delegation policies.*) *The board needs to judge whether the CEO's assertions are valid. It may do so by attempting to discover what these results cost other organizations to produce. This way it can decide whether it is demanding performance that cannot be accomplished with available funds. If the board determines that it has asked for more than is possible, it should redefine ends to be more achievable. Conversely, if the board determines that the desired results are achievable within available resources, it should reaffirm its existing Ends policies and expect the CEO to produce those results.*

4. If the action you propose involves a possible board policy change:

4a. What amendments or additions do you suggest? *The board may decide that it should require less ambitious ends.*

4b. What further information, if any, does the board need before deciding on this change? *Information about costs is essential.*

You are now ready for full board discussion and decision.

Rehearsal 3.17

TITLE: Who Builds the Building?

SCENARIO: The board and staff agree that a $6 million building relocation and expansion is needed in order for the organization to accomplish its ends. The board wants to be involved in where to build, how square footage will be allocated, design and materials, and other details. There is a great deal of confusion over what role the staff and board should have in the decision process. How should the board resolve this?

Resolve this scenario by answering the following questions:

1. What has the board already said in its relevant policies?

   Ends:

   Executive Limitations:

   Board-Management Delegation:

   Governance Process:

2. According to the board's policies, does this scenario refer to anything that has been delegated to the CEO?

   (*circle*)   Yes   No

   IF YES:

   2a. Does this scenario suggest that the CEO is in compliance with a reasonable interpretation of the board's Ends and Executive Limitations policies?

   (*circle*)   Yes   No   Unsure

   (*Explain your answer.*)

IF NO:

2b. Does this scenario reflect behavior consistent with the board's Governance Process and Board-Management Delegation policies?

(*circle*)   Yes   No   Unsure

(*Explain your answer.*)

3. What action, if any, should the board or board member now take? (*Specify the board or board member actions that you believe would be consistent with Governance Process and Board-Management Delegation policies.*)

4. If the action you propose involves a possible board policy change:

4a. What amendments or additions do you suggest?

4b. What further information, if any, does the board need before deciding on this change?

You are now ready for full board discussion and decision.

REHEARSAL WORKSHEET

Rehearsal 3.17

TITLE: Who Builds the Building?

SCENARIO: The board and staff agree that a $6 million building relocation and expansion is needed in order for the organization to accomplish its ends. The board wants to be involved in where to build, how square footage will be allocated, design and materials, and other details. There is a great deal of confusion over what role the staff and board should have in the decision process. How should the board resolve this?

Resolve this scenario by answering the following questions:

1. What has the board already said in its relevant policies?

   Ends: *N/A*

   Executive Limitations: *The CEO shall not allow any activity, decision, or circumstance that is imprudent (2.0); allow development of fiscal jeopardy or deviation of expenditures from Ends priorities (2.3.); acquire, encumber, or dispose of real property (2.3.8); make any purchase of over a specific dollar amount without a stringent method of ensuring the balance of long-term quality and cost (2.6.5); neglect to submit unbiased decision information required periodically by the board (2.8.3); or let the board be unaware of material internal and external changes (2.8.4).*

   Board-Management Delegation: *The board will develop Ends and Executive Limitations policies from the most general to more defined levels (3.3.1). The board will never prescribe organizational means (3.3.2). CEO decisions that are a reasonable interpretation of these policies "shall have full force and authority as if decided by the board" (3.3.3).*

   Governance Process: *The board will emphasize strategic leadership more than administrative detail (4.1). The board will direct and control the organization through written policies, with the major focus on intended impacts, not on administrative or programmatic means of attaining those effects (4.1.2). The board has direct responsibility for decision areas that Executive Limitations policies have denied to the CEO (4.2 notation).*

2. According to the board's policies, does this scenario refer to anything that has been delegated to the CEO?

   (circle)   Yes No

   The CEO is delegated responsibility for operational decisions, excepting those proscribed in Executive Limitations (for example, not acquiring "real property").

IF YES:

2a. Does this scenario suggest that the CEO is in compliance with a reasonable interpretation of the board's Ends and Executive Limitations policies?

(*circle*)   Yes   No   (Unsure)

(*Explain your answer.*) *The CEO may not make decisions about acquiring real property. Policies do not, however, prohibit the CEO from deciding about space allocations, furnishings, and some elements of design. The CEO would need to make an interpretation determining whether, for example, movable walls are or are not "real property."*

IF NO:

2b. Does this scenario reflect behavior consistent with the board's Governance Process and Board-Management Delegation policies?

(*circle*)   Yes   No   Unsure

(*Explain your answer.*)

3. What action, if any, should the board or board member now take? (*Specify the board or board member actions that you believe would be consistent with Governance Process and Board-Management Delegation policies.*) *The board has an obligation to support any reasonable CEO interpretation. Any elements of the project that are reasonably interpreted by the CEO not to be real property would be for the CEO and staff to decide. Any other property decisions are for the board to make. If the board has project-specific concerns about the CEO's decision-making authority, it can enact Executive Limitations policies especially for the project.*

4. If the action you propose involves a possible board policy change:

4a. What amendments or additions do you suggest? *Temporary policy changes regarding this scenario could be in effect for the duration of this building project. These could include Governance Process policies regarding criteria for land or building acquisition; Executive Limitations policies addressing whatever concerns the board has, ranging from cost and financing to use of certain materials or vendors; or Board-Management Delegation policies in which the board may adjust the methods and frequency of monitoring CEO performance (3.4) in order to ensure confidence that authority delegated has been well used.*

4b. What further information, if any, does the board need before deciding on this change? *The board may choose to engage a construction consultant to assist in making appropriate policies to guide its own work and the work of its CEO.*

You are now ready for full board discussion and decision.

Rehearsal 3.18

TITLE: Who Makes Important Decisions?

SCENARIO: The CEO of a for-profit corporation has a crucial decision to make regarding selection of a major distributor. The board is uncomfortable about the CEO's making a decision of this magnitude, as it considers this to be the single largest decision affecting profitability for shareholders. What should the board do?

Resolve this scenario by answering the following questions:

1. What has the board already said in its relevant policies?

   Ends:

   Executive Limitations:

   Board-Management Delegation:

   Governance Process:

2. According to the board's policies, does this scenario refer to anything that has been delegated to the CEO?

   (*circle*)   Yes   No

   IF YES:

   2a. Does this scenario suggest that the CEO is in compliance with a reasonable interpretation of the board's Ends and Executive Limitations policies?

   (*circle*)   Yes   No   Unsure

   (*Explain your answer.*)

IF NO:

2b. Does this scenario reflect behavior consistent with the board's Governance Process and Board-Management Delegation policies?

(*circle*)   Yes   No   Unsure

(*Explain your answer.*)

3. What action, if any, should the board or board member now take? (*Specify the board or board member actions that you believe would be consistent with Governance Process and Board-Management Delegation policies.*)

4. If the action you propose involves a possible board policy change:

4a. What amendments or additions do you suggest?

4b. What further information, if any, does the board need before deciding on this change?

You are now ready for full board discussion and decision.

REHEARSAL WORKSHEET

Rehearsal 3.18

TITLE: Who Makes Important Decisions?

SCENARIO: The CEO of a for-profit corporation has a crucial decision to make regarding selection of a major distributor. The board is uncomfortable about the CEO's making a decision of this magnitude, as it considers this to be the single largest decision affecting profitability for shareholders. What should the board do?

Resolve this scenario by answering the following questions:

1. What has the board already said in its relevant policies?

    Ends: *"The ultimate aim is return on shareholder equity better than the return for firms with similar risk characteristics" (1.0, example B).*

    Executive Limitations: *The CEO must not allow any activity, decision, or circumstance that is imprudent (2.0) or let the board be unaware of material internal and external changes (2.8.4).*

    Board-Management Delegation: *Successful CEO performance is defined as achievement of the ends and compliance with the Executive Limitations (3.2). The board will never prescribe organizational means delegated to the CEO (3.3.2). Decisions by the CEO that are a reasonable interpretation of these policies "shall have full force and authority as if decided by the board" (3.3.3).*

    Governance Process: *The board will emphasize strategic leadership more than administrative detail (4.1). The board will direct and control the organization through written policies, with the major focus on intended impacts, not on administrative or programmatic means of attaining those effects (4.1.2).*

2. According to the board's policies, does this scenario refer to anything that has been delegated to the CEO?

    (circle)   Yes   No

    The CEO's job is to make operational decisions that are a reasonable interpretation of the board's Ends and Executive Limitations policies.

IF YES:

2a. Does this scenario suggest that the CEO is in compliance with a reasonable interpretation of the board's Ends and Executive Limitations policies?

(*circle*) (Yes) No Unsure

(*Explain your answer.*) *The board's discomfort is indicated as relating to the magnitude of the decision. There is no indication that this is due to poor interpretations or judgments by the CEO.*

IF NO:

2b. Does this scenario reflect behavior consistent with the board's Governance Process and Board-Management Delegation policies?

(*circle*) Yes No Unsure

(*Explain your answer.*)

3. What action, if any, should the board or board member now take? (*Specify the board or board member actions that you believe would be consistent with Governance Process and Board-Management Delegation policies.*) *The board should recognize that CEOs are vested with innumerable decisions that affect profitability. As the selection of a vendor is purely a means issue, the board should ensure that its policies address what would constitute an unacceptable decision. If the board violates its "never prescribe means" policy, it loses its ability to hold the CEO accountable for profitable corporate performance.*

4. If the action you propose involves a possible board policy change:

4a. What amendments or additions do you suggest? *The board may choose to add Executive Limitations policies prohibiting certain circumstances regarding distributor selection.*

4b. What further information, if any, does the board need before deciding on this change? *The board should identify if there are unacceptable circumstances regarding distributor selection that are not addressed by existing Executive Limitations policies. For example, a board may wish to prohibit the use of distributors with a reliable track record of less than five years, less than a certain level of capitalization, or product unfamiliarity.*

You are now ready for full board discussion and decision.

Rehearsal 3.19

TITLE: Whose CEO Is It Anyway?

SCENARIO: The school board is made aware that at least part of the community is dissatisfied with the performance of the school system. Vocal community members have expressed their belief that the system's CEO should be replaced. How should the board respond?

Resolve this scenario by answering the following questions:

1. What has the board already said in its relevant policies?

    Ends:

    Executive Limitations:

    Board-Management Delegation:

    Governance Process:

2. According to the board's policies, does this scenario refer to anything that has been delegated to the CEO?

    (*circle*)   Yes   No

    IF YES:

    2a. Does this scenario suggest that the CEO is in compliance with a reasonable interpretation of the board's Ends and Executive Limitations policies?

    (*circle*)   Yes   No   Unsure

    (*Explain your answer.*)

IF NO:

2b. Does this scenario reflect behavior consistent with the board's Governance Process and Board-Management Delegation policies?

(*circle*) Yes No Unsure

(*Explain your answer.*)

3. What action, if any, should the board or board member now take? (*Specify the board or board member actions that you believe would be consistent with Governance Process and Board-Management Delegation policies.*)

4. If the action you propose involves a possible board policy change:

4a. What amendments or additions do you suggest?

4b. What further information, if any, does the board need before deciding on this change?

You are now ready for full board discussion and decision.

REHEARSAL WORKSHEET

Rehearsal 3.19

TITLE: Whose CEO Is It Anyway?

SCENARIO: The school board is made aware that at least part of the community is dissatisfied with the performance of the school system. Vocal community members have expressed their belief that the system's CEO should be replaced. How should the board respond?

Resolve this scenario by answering the following questions:

1. What has the board already said in its relevant policies?

    Ends: *Policy 1.0, example C*

    Executive Limitations: *All*

    Board-Management Delegation: *The board will view CEO performance as identical to organizational performance so that organizational accomplishment of board-stated ends and avoidance of board-proscribed means will be viewed as successful CEO performance (3.2.3). As long as the CEO uses any reasonable interpretation, the CEO is authorized to make all further decisions, which will have full force and authority as if decided by the board (3.3.3). Monitoring will be solely against Ends and Executive Limitations (3.4).*

    Governance Process: *The board, on behalf of the owners, sees to it that the school system accomplishes ends and avoids unacceptable means(4.0). The board will govern lawfully, emphasizing encouragement of diversity in viewpoints (4.1). Specific job outputs of the board, as an informed agent of the ownership, are those that ensure appropriate organizational performance (4.2). The board will include in its agenda plan consultations with selected groups within the ownership or other methods of gaining ownership input (4.3.2.A). The board will receive education on governance and on ends determination (4.3.2.B).*

2. According to the board's policies, does this scenario refer to anything that has been delegated to the CEO?

    (circle) (Yes) No

    The CEO is delegated responsibility for performance of the school system, as defined by Ends and Executive Limitations policies.

IF YES:

2a. Does this scenario suggest that the CEO is in compliance with a reasonable interpretation of the board's Ends and Executive Limitations policies?

(*circle*) Yes No (Unsure)

(*Explain your answer.*) *CEO performance has been questioned. Board members should confirm whether the board's monitoring demonstrates that the CEO has met the board's Ends and Executive Limitations expectations.*

IF NO:

2b. Does this scenario reflect behavior consistent with the board's Governance Process and Board-Management Delegation policies?

(*circle*) Yes No Unsure

(*Explain your answer.*)

3. What action, if any, should the board or board member now take? (*Specify the board or board member actions that you believe would be consistent with Governance Process and Board-Management Delegation policies.*) *If the board finds that CEO performance is a reasonable interpretation of board policies, the board has an obligation to support and defend the CEO. If the board has tolerated unacceptable performance, it must be more rigorous in demanding a reasonable interpretation of its policies. Replacement of the CEO should occur only if the CEO failed to meet the board's, not the community's, expectations.*

   The board should understand that while it cannot satisfy all opinion groups, it has an obligation to be aware of their opinions. Even if the school system is meeting board expectations, the board must consider whether the expectations themselves sufficiently reflect community values or needs.

   The board should include in its community linkage the goal of ensuring community understanding that dissatisfaction with board decisions should be brought to the board, not reflected in judgments of CEO performance.

4. If the action you propose involves a possible board policy change:

   4a. What amendments or additions do you suggest? *The board may find it useful to have a more detailed agenda plan to meet with community groups (4.3.2.A).*

   4b. What further information, if any, does the board need before deciding on this change? *The board should identify the groups not yet heard from that would add to the diversity of opinions the board can hear.*

   You are now ready for full board discussion and decision.

REHEARSAL WORKSHEET

Rehearsal 3.20

TITLE: If the CEO Didn't Know, Is He Still Accountable?

SCENARIO: A board discovers that there has been a serious problem with the financial systems. The board addresses this problem with the CEO. The CEO excuses himself, saying that he was not aware of the problem and thus cannot be held accountable for it. How should the board react?

Resolve this scenario by answering the following questions:

1. What has the board already said in its relevant policies?

   Ends:

   Executive Limitations:

   Board-Management Delegation:

   Governance Process:

2. According to the board's policies, does this scenario refer to anything that has been delegated to the CEO?

   (*circle*)   Yes   No

   IF YES:

   2a. Does this scenario suggest that the CEO is in compliance with a reasonable interpretation of the board's Ends and Executive Limitations policies?

   (*circle*)   Yes   No   Unsure

   (*Explain your answer.*)

IF NO:

2b. Does this scenario reflect behavior consistent with the board's Governance Process and Board-Management Delegation policies?

(*circle*)   Yes   No   Unsure

(*Explain your answer.*)

3. What action, if any, should the board or board member now take? (*Specify the board or board member actions that you believe would be consistent with Governance Process and Board-Management Delegation policies.*)

4. If the action you propose involves a possible board policy change:

4a. What amendments or additions do you suggest?

4b. What further information, if any, does the board need before deciding on this change?

You are now ready for full board discussion and decision.

REHEARSAL WORKSHEET

Rehearsal 3.20

TITLE: If the CEO Didn't Know, Is He Still Accountable?

SCENARIO: A board discovers that there has been a serious problem with the financial systems. The board addresses this problem with the CEO. The CEO excuses himself, saying that he was not aware of the problem and thus cannot be held accountable for it. How should the board react?

Resolve this scenario by answering the following questions:

1. What has the board already said in its relevant policies?

   Ends: *N/A*

   Executive Limitations: *The CEO shall not allow any organizational circumstance that is imprudent (2.0); risk fiscal jeopardy (2.3); allow corporate assets to be unprotected or unnecessarily risked (2.6); receive, process, or disburse funds under controls that are insufficient to meet the board-appointed auditor's standards (2.6.7); or fail to report in a timely manner any actual or anticipated noncompliance with any policy of the board (2.8.2).*

   Board-Management Delegation: *Monitoring will be solely against Ends and Executive Limitations (3.4). In monitoring CEO performance, the board will judge the reasonableness of the CEO's interpretation and whether data demonstrate accomplishment of the interpretation (3.4.3). The board will always judge with a "reasonable person" test (3.4.4).*

   Governance Process: *The board, on behalf of the owners, sees to it that the organization accomplishes ends and avoids unacceptable actions and situations (4.0). The board assures successful organizational performance on Ends and Executive Limitations. CEO monitoring will be included on the agenda if monitoring reports show policy violations or if policy criteria are to be debated (4.3.4). Outside monitoring assistance will be arranged so that the board can exercise confident control over organizational performance. This includes, but is not limited to, fiscal audit (4.8.1.B).*

2. According to the board's policies, does this scenario refer to anything that has been delegated to the CEO?

   (circle) No

   The CEO is delegated accountability for the organization's finances subject to the proscriptions outlined in Executive Limitations.

IF YES:

2a. Does this scenario suggest that the CEO is in compliance with a reasonable interpretation of the board's Ends and Executive Limitations policies?

(*circle*)   Yes   (No)   Unsure

(*Explain your answer.*) *At the broadest level, a serious problem with financial systems is an organizational circumstance that is imprudent. The board has added much greater specificity regarding unacceptable financial situations in its financial condition and asset protection policies, which appear to have been violated.*

IF NO:

2b. Does this scenario reflect behavior consistent with the board's Governance Process and Board-Management Delegation policies?

(*circle*)   Yes   No   Unsure

(*Explain your answer.*)

3. What action, if any, should the board or board member now take? (*Specify the board or board member actions that you believe would be consistent with Governance Process and Board-Management Delegation policies.*) *The board should note that it has outlined its expectations for organizational performance (Ends and Executive Limitations policies) and has delegated sufficient authority to the CEO to justify holding him accountable for such performance. The board can therefore assert that the CEO is the individual accountable for organizational failure even if he had no immediate personal knowledge of it or direct involvement in it. Accordingly, the CEO's explanation that he cannot be held accountable due to lack of awareness of the problem should be deemed unacceptable by the board.*

The CEO's lack of understanding of his accountability should be very troubling to the board. If the board has a reason to believe (through monitoring) that the CEO had inadequate systems to protect the organization against financial problems, the board also has a reason to consider replacing the CEO. On the other hand, if the board finds that the problem occurred despite reasonable steps to ensure compliance with board policy, it may decide that the CEO, while accountable, will not be blamed or penalized.

4. If the action you propose involves a possible board policy change:

4a. What amendments or additions do you suggest?

4b. What further information, if any, does the board need before deciding on this change?

You are now ready for full board discussion and decision.

Chapter 4

Rehearsal Scenarios: Board Member Interactions with the CEO or Staff

THE SCENARIOS in this chapter deal with issues that commonly arise between board members *as individuals* and the CEO or staff. In such board member-CEO interactions the Policy Governance board member must recall that no individual board member has the authority to instruct or evaluate the CEO or the staff. While there is no problem in people talking with each other, the key here is to remember that the communications must be firmly rooted in an understanding of the lack of individual authority of board members. In this chapter, you rehearse finding the Policy Governance principles about this issue in your policy manual—or the manual found in Resource 3—and applying them to the scenarios presented.

Rehearsal 4.1

TITLE: Program Decisions: Board or Staff?

SCENARIO: A credit union board member has an idea about a children's banking program that he thinks should be implemented. He shared it with the CEO, but the CEO did not proceed to implement the program. What should the board member do?

Resolve this scenario by answering the following questions:

1. What has the board already said in its relevant policies?

   Ends:

   Executive Limitations:

   Board-Management Delegation:

   Governance Process:

2. According to the board's policies, does this scenario refer to anything that has been delegated to the CEO?

   (*circle*)   Yes   No

   IF YES:

2a. Does this scenario suggest that the CEO is in compliance with a reasonable interpretation of the board's Ends and Executive Limitations policies?

   (*circle*)   Yes   No   Unsure

   (*Explain your answer.*)

IF NO:

2b. Does this scenario reflect behavior consistent with the board's Governance Process and Board-Management Delegation policies?

(*circle*)   Yes   No   Unsure

(*Explain your answer.*)

3. What action, if any, should the board or board member now take? (*Specify the board or board member actions that you believe would be consistent with Governance Process and Board-Management Delegation policies.*)

4. If the action you propose involves a possible board policy change:

4a. What amendments or additions do you suggest?

4b. What further information, if any, does the board need before deciding on this change?

You are now ready for full board discussion and decision.

Rehearsal 4.1

TITLE: Program Decisions: Board or Staff?

SCENARIO: A credit union board member has an idea about a children's banking program that he thinks should be implemented. He shared it with the CEO, but the CEO did not proceed to implement the program. What should the board member do?

Resolve this scenario by answering the following questions.

1. What has the board already said in its relevant policies?

   Ends: *"Savings of minor members will yield interest at a rate better than that available to other members" (1.0, example A).*

   Executive Limitations: *N/A*

   Board-Management Delegation: *Only decisions of the board are binding on the CEO (3.1). Decisions or instructions of board members are not binding unless specifically authorized (3.1.1). The board instructs the CEO through Ends and Executive Limitations policies, allowing the CEO to use any reasonable interpretation of these policies (3.3), in which case the CEO is authorized to establish all further policies, practices, decisions, activities, and so on (3.3.3). As long as a particular delegation is in place, the board will respect and support the CEO's choices (3.3.4).*

   Governance Process: *The purpose of the board is to ensure achievement of ends and avoidance of unacceptable actions and situations (4.0). The board will observe Policy Governance principles, with emphasis on strategic leadership more than on administrative detail and collective decisions rather than individual decisions (4.1). The board will focus on intended long-term impacts outside the organization, not on the administrative or programmatic means of attaining those effects (4.1.2). The board establishes Ends policies and Executive Limitations, which establish the boundaries within which all executive activity and decisions must take place (4.2.2). A board member may recommend or request an item to be on the agenda for board discussion (4.3.2.C). Board members' interaction with the CEO must recognize the lack of authority vested in individuals except when explicitly board authorized (4.5.3.A).*

2. According to the board's policies, does this scenario refer to anything that has been delegated to the CEO?

   (*circle*)   Yes   No

   The determination of operational means, including banking programs is delegated to the CEO.

IF YES:

2a. Does this scenario suggest that the CEO is in compliance with a reasonable interpretation of the board's Ends and Executive Limitations policies?

(*circle*)   (Yes)   No   Unsure

(*Explain your answer.*) *There is no reason to believe that the CEO is not complying with board policy.*

IF NO:

2b. Does this scenario reflect behavior consistent with the board's Governance Process and Board-Management Delegation policies?

(*circle*)   Yes   No   Unsure

(*Explain your answer.*)

3. What action, if any, should the board or board member now take? (*Specify the board or board member actions that you believe would be consistent with Governance Process and Board-Management Delegation policies.*) *The board member with the program idea must remember that the CEO is free to accept or reject suggestions and that as an individual, he has no authority over the CEO. He should also remember that even the board is committed to not prescribing operational means. If he feels that the board's Ends policy is either inappropriate or open to an unacceptable range of interpretation, he can request that the board consider an amendment to it. If the board member feels that the credit union should produce results for minors beyond those included in Ends policies, he can request that the board consider such an addition.*

4. If the action you propose involves a possible board policy change:

4a. What amendments or additions do you suggest? *The board member may propose that the board consider defining Ends policies prescribing some identified additional results for minors.*

4b. What further information, if any, does the board need before deciding on this change? *If there is a proposal to revise the Ends policies to expand the benefits to be received by minors, the board should collect information regarding the cost and desirability of achieving this prospective outcome.*

You are now ready for full board discussion and decision.

Rehearsal 4.2

TITLE: CEO Input: To the Board or to Certain Members?

SCENARIO: The CEO is lobbying board members with whom he is personally close to make ends decisions that he favors. What should the board members do?

Resolve this scenario by answering the following questions:

1. What has the board already said in its relevant policies?

   Ends:

   Executive Limitations:

   Board-Management Delegation:

   Governance Process:

2. According to the board's policies, does this scenario refer to anything that has been delegated to the CEO?

   (*circle*)   Yes   No

   IF YES:

   2a. Does this scenario suggest that the CEO is in compliance with a reasonable interpretation of the board's Ends and Executive Limitations policies?

   (*circle*)   Yes   No   Unsure

   (*Explain your answer.*)

IF NO:

2b. Does this scenario reflect behavior consistent with the board's Governance Process and Board-Management Delegation policies?

(*circle*)   Yes   No   Unsure

(*Explain your answer.*)

3. What action, if any, should the board or board member now take? (*Specify the board or board member actions that you believe would be consistent with Governance Process and Board-Management Delegation policies.*)

4. If the action you propose involves a possible board policy change:

4a. What amendments or additions do you suggest?

4b. What further information, if any, does the board need before deciding on this change?

You are now ready for full board discussion and decision.

Rehearsal 4.2

TITLE: CEO Input: To the Board or to Certain Members?

SCENARIO: The CEO is lobbying board members with whom he is personally close to make ends decisions that he favors. What should the board members do?

Resolve this scenario by answering the following questions.

1. What has the board already said in its relevant policies?

   Ends: *N/A*

   Executive Limitations: *The CEO may not neglect to submit unbiased information (2.8.3). The CEO may not fail to deal with the board as a whole (2.8.8).*

   Board-Management Delegation: *The board establishes Ends policies, allowing the CEO to use any reasonable interpretation of these policies (3.3). Adherence to the applicable Executive Limitations policy is to be monitored by direct inspection (3.4.5).*

   Governance Process: *The purpose of the board is to make policy on behalf of the owners, not the staff (4.0). The board initiates policy, rather than reacting to staff (4.1.1). The board as a body will listen to ends input from the staff (4.3.2.B). Board members' loyalty to the ownership must be unconflicted by loyalties to staff (4.5.1).*

2. According to the board's policies, does this scenario refer to anything that has been delegated to the CEO?

   (circle) (Yes) No

   The CEO is instructed not to fail to deal with the board as a body.

   IF YES:

   2a. Does this scenario suggest that the CEO is in compliance with a reasonable interpretation of the board's Ends and Executive Limitations policies?

   (circle) Yes (No) Unsure

   (Explain your answer.) The CEO has the right to talk to anyone but has violated the expectation that when dealing with official business of the board he must deal with the entire board.

IF NO:

2b. Does this scenario reflect behavior consistent with the board's Governance Process and Board-Management Delegation policies?

(*circle*)　　Yes　　No　　Unsure

(*Explain your answer.*)

3. What action, if any, should the board or board member now take? (*Specify the board or board member actions that you believe would be consistent with Governance Process and Board-Management Delegation policies.*) *The board members being lobbied by the CEO should remind the CEO that the board has committed itself to hearing staff input about ends and that the CEO is expected to deal with the board as a whole. The board members should remind themselves that the policies they make are to be made on behalf of the owners, not the staff. When the board monitors its Executive Limitations policy 2.8, note should be made of the CEO's violation of 2.8.3 and 2.8.8.*

4. If the action you propose involves a possible board policy change:

4a. What amendments or additions do you suggest?

4b. What further information, if any, does the board need before deciding on this change?

You are now ready for full board discussion and decision.

Rehearsal 4.3

TITLE: How Do I Get More Information?

SCENARIO: A board member keeps asking the CEO for detailed reports regarding operations. The information required does not pertain to any Ends or Executive Limitations policies. The CEO has refused to supply the reports, stating that it would take too many staff hours to produce them. What should the board member do?

Resolve this scenario by answering the following questions:

1. What has the board already said in its relevant policies?

    Ends:

    Executive Limitations:

    Board-Management Delegation:

    Governance Process:

2. According to the board's policies, does this scenario refer to anything that has been delegated to the CEO?

    (*circle*)   Yes   No

    IF YES:

    2a. Does this scenario suggest that the CEO is in compliance with a reasonable interpretation of the board's Ends and Executive Limitations policies?

    (*circle*)   Yes   No   Unsure

    (*Explain your answer.*)

IF NO:

2b. Does this scenario reflect behavior consistent with the board's Governance Process and Board-Management Delegation policies?

(*circle*)   Yes   No   Unsure

(*Explain your answer.*)

3. What action, if any, should the board or board member now take? (*Specify the board or board member actions that you believe would be consistent with Governance Process and Board-Management Delegation policies.*)

4. If the action you propose involves a possible board policy change:

4a. What amendments or additions do you suggest?

4b. What further information, if any, does the board need before deciding on this change?

You are now ready for full board discussion and decision.

Rehearsal 4.3

TITLE: How Do I Get More Information?

SCENARIO: A board member keeps asking the CEO for detailed reports regarding operations. The information required does not pertain to any Ends or Executive Limitations policies. The CEO has refused to supply the reports, stating that it would take too many staff hours to produce them. What should the board member do?

Resolve this scenario by answering the following questions:

1. What has the board already said in its relevant policies?

   Ends: *N/A*

   Executive Limitations: *The CEO may not allow the board to be uninformed (2.8); neglect to submit information required by the board or let the board be unaware of relevant trends (2.8.3) or of significant incidental information, material internal changes, and the like (2.8.4); fail to advise the board if it is not in compliance with its own policies, particularly in the case of board behavior detrimental to the board-CEO work relationship (2.8.5); or fail to deal with the board as a whole except when fulfilling requests for information (2.8.6).*

   Board-Management Delegation: *Only decisions of the board are binding on the CEO (3.1). Decisions or instructions of individual board members are not binding unless specifically authorized by the board (3.1.1). The CEO can refuse a board member's request for information or assistance if such a request requires "a material amount of staff time or funds or is disruptive" (3.1.2). CEO performance will be monitored and judged only against the board's Ends and Executive Limitations policies (3.4). Information that does not address board policies will not be considered when monitoring CEO performance (3.4.1).*

   Governance Process: *The board will govern with an emphasis on collective (not individual) decisions (4.1). The board is responsible for ensuring successful organizational performance on Ends and Executive Limitations (4.2.3). Board members may request items for board discussion (4.3.2.C). The board is committed to proper use of authority (4.5). Board members may not attempt to exercise individual authority over the organization (4.5.3). Board members must recognize the lack of authority vested in individuals (4.5.3.A).*

2. According to the board's policies, does this scenario refer to anything that has been delegated to the CEO?

   (*circle*)   (Yes)   No

   The CEO has been expected to deal with the board as a body and to provide the board with the information it has said it requires in Executive Limitations policy 2.8.

   IF YES:

   2a. Does this scenario suggest that the CEO is in compliance with a reasonable interpretation of the board's Ends and Executive Limitations policies?

   (*circle*)   (Yes)   No   Unsure

   (*Explain your answer.*) *There is no reason to believe that the CEO has not provided the board with the information it required. To remain in compliance, the CEO may find it necessary to inform the board that board member behavior inconsistent with board policies is disruptive.*

   IF NO:

   2b. Does this scenario reflect behavior consistent with the board's Governance Process and Board-Management Delegation policies?

   (*circle*)   Yes   No   Unsure

   (*Explain your answer.*)

3. What action, if any, should the board or board member now take? (*Specify the board or board member actions that you believe would be consistent with Governance Process and Board-Management Delegation policies.*) *The board member should remind himself that the board has stated that while the board can get any information it requests, board members may be refused information if fulfilling their request would consume more resources than the CEO thinks are reasonable. The board as a body should respond to CEO feedback about the problem by reinforcing its determination to protect the CEO from individual board member requests.*

4. If the action you propose involves a possible board policy change:

   4a. What amendments or additions do you suggest?

   4b. What further information, if any, does the board need before deciding on this change?

   You are now ready for full board discussion and decision.

Rehearsal 4.4

TITLE: Should Board Members Influence Vendor Selection?

SCENARIO: A vendor disgruntled about not being invited to bid on a contract calls an influential board member and complains. What should the board member do?

Resolve this scenario by answering the following questions:

1. What has the board already said in its relevant policies?

   Ends:

   Executive Limitations:

   Board-Management Delegation:

   Governance Process:

2. According to the board's policies, does this scenario refer to anything that has been delegated to the CEO?

   (*circle*)   Yes   No

   IF YES:

   2a. Does this scenario suggest that the CEO is in compliance with a reasonable interpretation of the board's Ends and Executive Limitations policies?

   (*circle*)   Yes   No   Unsure

   (*Explain your answer.*)

IF NO:

2b. Does this scenario reflect behavior consistent with the board's Governance Process and Board-Management Delegation policies?

(*circle*)   Yes   No   Unsure

(*Explain your answer.*)

3. What action, if any, should the board or board member now take? (*Specify the board or board member actions that you believe would be consistent with Governance Process and Board-Management Delegation policies.*)

4. If the action you propose involves a possible board policy change:

4a. What amendments or additions do you suggest?

4b. What further information, if any, does the board need before deciding on this change?

You are now ready for full board discussion and decision.

REHEARSAL WORKSHEET

Rehearsal 4.4

TITLE: Should Board Members Influence Vendor Selection?

SCENARIO: A vendor disgruntled about not being invited to bid on a contract calls an influential board member and complains. What should the board member do?

Resolve this scenario by answering the following questions.

1. What has the board already said in its relevant policies?

   Ends: *N/A*

   Executive Limitations: *The CEO shall not cause or allow circumstances that are contrary to commonly accepted business and professional ethics and practices (2.0); make any purchase for which normally prudent protection has not been given against conflicts of interest or of over a specified number of dollars without having obtained comparative prices and quality or of over a specified number of dollars without a stringent method of ensuring the balance of long-term quality or cost (2.6.5).*

   Board-Management Delegation: *As long as the CEO uses any reasonable interpretation of the board's Ends and Executive Limitations policies, the CEO may make all further decisions (3.3.3). The standard for compliance shall be any reasonable CEO interpretation (3.4.4).*

   Governance Process: *A board member may recommend or request an item for board discussion (4.3.2.C). Board members must disclose their involvements with vendors that might constitute a conflict (4.5.2.A). Board members may not attempt to exercise individual authority over the organization (4.5.3). Members' interaction with the CEO or with staff must recognize the lack of authority vested in individuals except when explicitly authorized by the board (4.5.3.A). Members' interactions with the public must recognize the inability of any board member to speak for the board (4.5.3.B).*

2. According to the board's policies, does this scenario refer to anything that has been delegated to the CEO?

   (*circle*)   Yes   No

   The CEO has the right to make purchasing decisions, subject to applicable Executive Limitations policy.

IF YES:

2a. Does this scenario suggest that the CEO is in compliance with a reasonable interpretation of the board's Ends and Executive Limitations policies?

(*circle*)   (Yes)   No   Unsure

(*Explain your answer.*) *There is no reason to believe that the CEO has violated board policy. Executive Limitations policy 2.6.5 does not dictate the vendors from whom bids must be obtained.*

IF NO:

2b. Does this scenario reflect behavior consistent with the board's Governance Process and Board-Management Delegation policies?

(*circle*)   Yes   No   Unsure

(*Explain your answer.*)

3. What action, if any, should the board or board member now take? (*Specify the board or board member actions that you believe would be consistent with Governance Process and Board-Management Delegation policies.*) *The board member should explain to the vendor that he or she has no authority to influence purchasing decisions and that indeed to do so would violate the board's expectations of ethical conduct. If the board member suspects that the CEO has a purchasing procedure that violates board policy, he or she may ask the board to undertake additional monitoring of that policy.*

4. If the action you propose involves a possible board policy change:

4a. What amendments or additions do you suggest?

4b. What further information, if any, does the board need before deciding on this change?

You are now ready for full board discussion and decision.

Rehearsal 4.5

TITLE: Do Board Members Have Authority over Staff?

SCENARIO: A board member instructs staff to perform tasks for her such as scheduling lunch appointments. Staff have cooperated with these requests, but now the CEO has instructed staff that this may not continue and has advised the board member of this instruction. What should the board member do?

Resolve this scenario by answering the following questions:

1. What has the board already said in its relevant policies?

   Ends:

   Executive Limitations:

   Board-Management Delegation:

   Governance Process:

2. According to the board's policies, does this scenario refer to anything that has been delegated to the CEO?

   (*circle*)   Yes   No

   IF YES:

   2a. Does this scenario suggest that the CEO is in compliance with a reasonable interpretation of the board's Ends and Executive Limitations policies?

   (*circle*)   Yes   No   Unsure

   (*Explain your answer.*)

IF NO:

2b. Does this scenario reflect behavior consistent with the board's Governance Process and Board-Management Delegation policies?

(*circle*)   Yes   No   Unsure

(*Explain your answer.*)

3. What action, if any, should the board or board member now take? (*Specify the board or board member actions that you believe would be consistent with Governance Process and Board-Management Delegation policies.*)

4. If the action you propose involves a possible board policy change:

4a. What amendments or additions do you suggest?

4b. What further information, if any, does the board need before deciding on this change?

You are now ready for full board discussion and decision.

Rehearsal 4.5

TITLE: Do Board Members Have Authority over Staff?

SCENARIO: A board member instructs staff to perform tasks for her such as scheduling lunch appointments. Staff have cooperated with these requests, but now the CEO has instructed staff that this may not continue and has advised the board member of this instruction. What should the board member do?

Resolve this scenario by answering the following questions:

1. What has the board already said in its relevant policies?

   Ends: *N/A*

   Executive Limitations: *The CEO may not allow circumstances that are unlawful, imprudent, or in violation of commonly accepted business ethics (2.0) or fail to advise the board if it is not in compliance with its own policies, particularly in the case of board behavior detrimental to the board-CEO work relationship (2.8.5).*

   Board-Management Delegation: *Only decisions of the board are binding on the CEO (3.1). Decisions or instructions of individual board members are not binding unless specifically authorized by the board (3.1.1). The CEO may refuse board members' requests for information or assistance if such requests are disruptive. (3.1.2).*

   Governance Process: *Board members may not attempt to exercise individual authority over the organization (4.5.3). The CGO's job is to ensure that the board behaves consistently with its own rules (4.4.1). The board commits itself and its members to ethical conduct, including proper use of authority and appropriate decorum (4.5). Board members may not attempt to exercise individual authority over the organization (4.5.3).*

2. According to the board's policies, does this scenario refer to anything that has been delegated to the CEO?

   (circle) (Yes) No

   The CEO has the job of ensuring organizational performance that reflects any reasonable interpretation of the board's Ends and Executive Limitations policies. The CEO is thus responsible for all staff actions.

IF YES:

2a. Does this scenario suggest that the CEO is in compliance with a reasonable interpretation of the board's Ends and Executive Limitations policies?

(*circle*)   (Yes)   No   Unsure

(*Explain your answer.*) *The CEO is exercising his prerogatives when instructing the staff. If the board member's behavior does not stop, the CEO should also consider advising the board of this board member's behavior, since it is detrimental to the board-CEO working relationship. This would be in compliance with Executive Limitations policy 2.8.5.*

IF NO:

2b. Does this scenario reflect behavior consistent with the board's Governance Process and Board-Management Delegation policies?

(*circle*)   Yes   No   Unsure

(*Explain your answer.*)

3. What action, if any, should the board or board member now take? (*Specify the board or board member actions that you believe would be consistent with Governance Process and Board-Management Delegation policies.*) *The board member should apologize and refrain from instructing the staff.*

4. If the action you propose involves a possible board policy change:

4a. What amendments or additions do you suggest?

4b. What further information, if any, does the board need before deciding on this change?

You are now ready for full board discussion and decision.

Rehearsal 4.6

TITLE: Does Policy Governance Preclude Board-Staff Dialogue?

SCENARIO: To preclude inappropriate discussions between board and staff members, the CEO prohibits staff members from socializing with board members in any context unless they first get permission from the CEO. Board members question the propriety of such a staff policy. What should they do?

Resolve this scenario by answering the following questions:

1. What has the board already said in its relevant policies?

    Ends:

    Executive Limitations:

    Board-Management Delegation:

    Governance Process:

2. According to the board's policies, does this scenario refer to anything that has been delegated to the CEO?

    (*circle*)   Yes   No

    IF YES:

2a. Does this scenario suggest that the CEO is in compliance with a reasonable interpretation of the board's Ends and Executive Limitations policies?

    (*circle*)   Yes   No   Unsure

    (*Explain your answer.*)

IF NO:

2b. Does this scenario reflect behavior consistent with the board's Governance Process and Board-Management Delegation policies?

(*circle*)   Yes   No   Unsure

(*Explain your answer.*)

3. What action, if any, should the board or board member now take? (*Specify the board or board member actions that you believe would be consistent with Governance Process and Board-Management Delegation policies.*)

4. If the action you propose involves a possible board policy change:

    4a. What amendments or additions do you suggest?

    4b. What further information, if any, does the board need before deciding on this change?

You are now ready for full board discussion and decision.

Rehearsal 4.6

TITLE: Does Policy Governance Preclude Board-Staff Dialogue?

SCENARIO: To preclude inappropriate discussions between board and staff members, the CEO prohibits staff members from socializing with board members in any context unless they first get permission from the CEO. Board members question the propriety of such a staff policy. What should they do?

Resolve this scenario by answering the following questions:

1. What has the board already said in its relevant policies?

   Ends: *N/A*

   Executive Limitations: *The CEO shall not cause or allow conditions that are unlawful, imprudent, or unethical (2.0). The CEO shall not cause or allow staff conditions that are unfair (2.2).*

   Board-Management Delegation: *The board will never give instructions to persons who report directly or indirectly to the CEO (3.2.1). The board will not evaluate, either formally or informally, any staff member other than the CEO (3.2.2). As long as the CEO uses any reasonable interpretation of the board's Ends and Executive Limitations policies, the CEO can make all further policies (3.3.3). The staff treatment policy is to be reviewed annually (3.4.5).*

   Governance Process: *Board members may not attempt to exercise individual authority over the organization (4.5.3). Board members will not express individual judgments of performance of employees of the CEO (4.5.3.C).*

2. According to the board's policies, does this scenario refer to anything that has been delegated to the CEO?

   (*circle*)   (Yes)   No

   The CEO is empowered to make all decisions regarding the staff, subject to applicable Executive Limitations policies.

IF YES:

2a. Does this scenario suggest that the CEO is in compliance with a reasonable interpretation of the board's Ends and Executive Limitations policies?

(*circle*)   Yes   (No)   Unsure

(*Explain your answer.*) *It is not likely that prohibiting interaction between staff members and board members is a reasonable interpretation of "unfair" or even "unlawful."*

IF NO:

2b. Does this scenario reflect behavior consistent with the board's Governance Process and Board-Management Delegation policies?

(*circle*)   Yes   No   Unsure

(*Explain your answer.*)

3. What action, if any, should the board or board member now take? (*Specify the board or board member actions that you believe would be consistent with Governance Process and Board-Management Delegation policies.*). *The concerned board members should have the matter placed on the board's agenda for discussion. If the board finds that the CEO's rule is a reasonable interpretation of its policy, yet the board finds the rule unacceptable, the board should amend its policy. If the board finds that the CEO's rule is not a reasonable interpretation of its policy, the CEO should be found in violation of the policy and should be expected to correct the situation. The board should also consider that the CEO may have established the rule in response to detrimental board behavior, such as board members' undermining CEO authority to the staff. In this case, the board's own discipline warrants attention, and the board should confirm its commitment to refrain from inappropriate staff instruction and evaluation.*

4. If the action you propose involves a possible board policy change:

4a. What amendments or additions do you suggest? *Executive limitations policy 2.2 may be amended with wording such as "although the authority to instruct and evaluate staff remains with the CEO, the CEO shall not prevent contact between the board or its members and the staff."*

4b. What further information, if any, does the board need before deciding on this change?

You are now ready for full board discussion and decision.

REHEARSAL WORKSHEET

Rehearsal 4.7

TITLE: Is This a "Reasonable Interpretation"?

SCENARIO: Reviewing an Executive Limitations monitoring report received in the mail, a board member questions whether the CEO's interpretation is in fact reasonable. How should she address her concern?

Resolve this scenario by answering the following questions:

1. What has the board already said in its relevant policies?

    Ends:

    Executive Limitations:

    Board-Management Delegation:

    Governance Process:

2. According to the board's policies, does this scenario refer to anything that has been delegated to the CEO?

    (*circle*)   Yes   No

    IF YES:

    2a. Does this scenario suggest that the CEO is in compliance with a reasonable interpretation of the board's Ends and Executive Limitations policies?

    (*circle*)   Yes   No   Unsure

    (*Explain your answer.*)

IF NO:

2b. Does this scenario reflect behavior consistent with the board's Governance Process and Board-Management Delegation policies?

(*circle*)   Yes   No   Unsure

(*Explain your answer.*)

3. What action, if any, should the board or board member now take? (*Specify the board or board member actions that you believe would be consistent with Governance Process and Board-Management Delegation policies.*)

4. If the action you propose involves a possible board policy change:

    4a. What amendments or additions do you suggest?

    4b. What further information, if any, does the board need before deciding on this change?

You are now ready for full board discussion and decision.

Rehearsal 4.7

TITLE: Is This a "Reasonable Interpretation"?

SCENARIO: Reviewing an Executive Limitations monitoring report received in the mail, a board member questions whether the CEO's interpretation is in fact reasonable. How should she address her concern?

Resolve this scenario by answering the following questions:

1. What has the board already said in its relevant policies?

   Ends: *N/A*

   Executive Limitations: *N/A*

   Board-Management Delegation: *Only decisions of the board are binding on the CEO (3.1). The board instructs the CEO through Ends and Executive Limitations policies, allowing the CEO to use any reasonable interpretation of these policies (3.3). When monitoring CEO performance, the board will judge the reasonableness of the CEO's interpretation and whether accomplishment of that interpretation was demonstrated (3.3.3). The board is the final arbiter of reasonableness but will always judge with a "reasonable person" test rather than with interpretations favored by board members or by the board as a whole (3.4.4).*

   Governance Process: *The board will govern with an emphasis on collective rather than individual decisions (4.1). The board is responsible for ensuring organizational performance on Ends and Executive Limitations (4.1.3). A board member may request an item for board discussion on the agenda (4.3.2.C). CEO monitoring will be on the agenda if monitoring reports show violations or policy criteria are to be debated (4.3.4). Board members must recognize their inability to speak for the board (4.5.3.B).*

2. According to the board's policies, does this scenario refer to anything that has been delegated to the CEO?

   (*circle*)   Yes   (No)

   IF YES:

2a. Does this scenario suggest that the CEO is in compliance with a reasonable interpretation of the board's Ends and Executive Limitations policies?

   (*circle*)   Yes   No   Unsure

   (*Explain your answer.*)

IF NO:

2b. Does this scenario reflect behavior consistent with the board's Governance Process and Board-Management Delegation policies?

(*circle*)   Yes   No   Unsure

(*Explain your answer.*) *Each board member must decide if the monitoring report it receives demonstrates a reasonable interpretation of board policy.*

3. What action, if any, should the board or board member now take? (*Specify the board or board member actions that you believe would be consistent with Governance Process and Board-Management Delegation policies.*) *The board member has the right to ask the CEO for information and should consider doing so. The board member will be aware that the board will review the latest monitoring reports at each board meeting, and the decision about the reasonableness of the CEO interpretation will be decided by the board as a whole. The board member should contact the CGO to inform him or her that it will likely be necessary to discuss the monitoring report in detail.*

4. If the action you propose involves a possible board policy change:

    4a. What amendments or additions do you suggest?

    4b. What further information, if any, does the board need before deciding on this change?

    You are now ready for full board discussion and decision.

Rehearsal 4.8

TITLE: Should Board Members Speak on Behalf of the CEO?

SCENARIO: An individual was hurt on the organization's property. The CEO submitted the liability claim to the insurance company and notified the board of the situation. A board member is contacted by a lawyer for the plaintiff, asking the board member questions about the safety history of the organization, as well as what he knows about the specific injury accident. What should he do?

Resolve this scenario by answering the following questions:

1. What has the board already said in its relevant policies?

   Ends:

   Executive Limitations:

   Board-Management Delegation:

   Governance Process:

2. According to the board's policies, does this scenario refer to anything that has been delegated to the CEO?

   (*circle*)   Yes   No

   IF YES:

   2a. Does this scenario suggest that the CEO is in compliance with a reasonable interpretation of the board's Ends and Executive Limitations policies?

   (*circle*)   Yes   No   Unsure

   (*Explain your answer.*)

IF NO:

2b. Does this scenario reflect behavior consistent with the board's Governance Process and Board-Management Delegation policies?

(*circle*)   Yes   No   Unsure

(*Explain your answer.*)

3. What action, if any, should the board or board member now take? (*Specify the board or board member actions that you believe would be consistent with Governance Process and Board-Management Delegation policies.*)

4. If the action you propose involves a possible board policy change:

4a. What amendments or additions do you suggest?

4b. What further information, if any, does the board need before deciding on this change?

You are now ready for full board discussion and decision.

REHEARSAL WORKSHEET

Rehearsal 4.8

TITLE: Should Board Members Speak on Behalf of the CEO?

SCENARIO: An individual was hurt on the organization's property. The CEO submitted the liability claim to the insurance company and notified the board of the situation. A board member is contacted by a lawyer for the plaintiff, asking the board member questions about the safety history of the organization, as well as what he knows about the specific injury accident. What should he do?

Resolve this scenario by answering the following questions:

1. What has the board already said in its relevant policies?

   Ends: *N/A*

   Executive Limitations: *The CEO may not fail to insure against liability losses (2.6.1) or let the board be uninformed or unaware of any significant information including threatened or pending lawsuits (2.8.4).*

   Board-Management Delegation: *The CEO is authorized to make all ends and operational means decisions as long as they are consistent with the board's Ends and Executive Limitations policies (3.3.3).*

   Governance Process: *Board members' interactions with the public, press, or other entities must recognize that they are unable to speak for the board (4.5.3.B). Board members will not express individual judgments of performance or employees of the CEO (4.5.3.C). Board members will respect the confidentiality appropriate to issues of a sensitive nature (4.5.4).*

2. According to the board's policies, does this scenario refer to anything that has been delegated to the CEO?

   (circle) (Yes) No

   The CEO is responsible for handling operational means issues, subject to applicable Executive Limitations policy.

IF YES:

2a. Does this scenario suggest that the CEO is in compliance with a reasonable interpretation of the board's Ends and Executive Limitations policies?

(*circle*)   (Yes)   No   Unsure

(*Explain your answer.*) *The CEO has informed the board, as required by Executive Limitations policy 2.8.4, and has insurance coverage, as required by Executive Limitations policy 2.6.1.*

IF NO:

2b. Does this scenario reflect behavior consistent with the board's Governance Process and Board-Management Delegation policies?

(*circle*)   Yes   No   Unsure

(*Explain your answer.*)

3. What action, if any, should the board or board member now take? (*Specify the board or board member actions that you believe would be consistent with Governance Process and Board-Management Delegation policies.*) *The board member should not respond to the lawyer's questions and should refer the lawyer to the CEO, since the CEO has authority to speak about and decide any reasonable interpretation of Ends and Executive Limitations policies. However, the board member may notice that while policy 4.5.3.B states that individual board members may not speak for the board, no policy stipulates explicitly that board members may not speak for the CEO. The board member should bring this omission to the board's attention for a possible policy amendment.*

4. If the action you propose involves a possible board policy change:

4a. What amendments or additions do you suggest? *The board should consider amending policy 4.5.3.B to add that board members do not have the authority to speak for the CEO.*

4b. What further information, if any, does the board need before deciding on this change?

You are now ready for full board discussion and decision.

Rehearsal 4.9

TITLE: Should Board Members Intervene in Staff Disputes?

SCENARIO: A board member gets a call from a staff member complaining about low staff morale. How should the board member respond?

Resolve this scenario by answering the following questions:

1. What has the board already said in its relevant policies?

   Ends:

   Executive Limitations:

   Board-Management Delegation:

   Governance Process:

2. According to the board's policies, does this scenario refer to anything that has been delegated to the CEO?

   (*circle*)   Yes   No

   IF YES:

   2a. Does this scenario suggest that the CEO is in compliance with a reasonable interpretation of the board's Ends and Executive Limitations policies?

   (*circle*)   Yes   No   Unsure

   (*Explain your answer.*)

IF NO:

2b. Does this scenario reflect behavior consistent with the board's Governance Process and Board-Management Delegation policies?

(*circle*)   Yes   No   Unsure

(*Explain your answer.*)

3. What action, if any, should the board or board member now take? (*Specify the board or board member actions that you believe would be consistent with Governance Process and Board-Management Delegation policies.*)

4. If the action you propose involves a possible board policy change:

4a. What amendments or additions do you suggest?

4b. What further information, if any, does the board need before deciding on this change?

You are now ready for full board discussion and decision.

REHEARSAL WORKSHEET

Rehearsal 4.9

TITLE: Should Board Members Intervene in Staff Disputes?

SCENARIO: A board member gets a call from a staff member complaining about low staff morale. How should the board member respond?

Resolve this scenario by answering the following questions:

1.   What has the board already said in its relevant policies?

Ends: *N/A*

Executive Limitations: *The CEO may not allow staff conditions that are unfair, undignified, disorganized, or unclear (2.2); operate without written rules that provide for effective handling of grievances (2.2.1); or fail to acquaint staff with the CEO's interpretation of their protections under this policy (2.2.3).*

Board-Management Delegation: *The board's sole official connection to operations is through the CEO (3.0). All authority and accountability of staff, as far as the board is concerned, are considered the authority and accountability of the CEO (3.2). The board will never give instructions to people who work for the CEO (3.2.1). The board will not evaluate any staff member other than the CEO (3.2.2). As long as the CEO complies with Ends and Executive Limitations policies, the board will respect and support the CEO's choices (3.3.4). The board can monitor any policy at any time (3.4.5).*

Governance Process: *The board will cultivate a sense of group responsibility (4.1). The board will have discipline regarding respect of roles (4.1.3). Board members' interactions with staff must recognize that individuals lack authority except when authorized by the board (4.5.3.A).*

2.   According to the board's policies, does this scenario refer to anything that has been delegated to the CEO?

(*circle*)   No

Personnel issues are under the control of the CEO, subject to applicable Executive Limitations policy.

IF YES:

2a. Does this scenario suggest that the CEO is in compliance with a reasonable interpretation of the board's Ends and Executive Limitations policies?

(*circle*)   Yes   No   (Unsure)

(*Explain your answer.*) *The Executive Limitations policies establish, at the broadest levels, appropriate standards regarding the treatment of staff. An allegation of low morale does not necessarily mean that these standards have been violated.*

IF NO:

2b. Does this scenario reflect behavior consistent with the board's Governance Process and Board-Management Delegation policies?

(*circle*)   Yes   No   Unsure

(*Explain your answer.*)

3. What action, if any, should the board or board member now take? (*Specify the board or board member actions that you believe would be consistent with Governance Process and Board-Management Delegation policies.*) *The board member should refer the staff member to the internal grievance system and may choose to tell the CEO that she has heard from a staff member who is unhappy with personnel conditions. The board member should note that the board has prohibited personnel decisions and personnel treatment that it regards as unacceptable. It did not and cannot require that staff feel a certain way. If the staff member alleges a violation of board policy, the board member can request that the board require an extra monitoring of policy 2.2. The board member should not attempt to intervene in the problems of individual staff members.*

4. If the action you propose involves a possible board policy change:

4a. What amendments or additions do you suggest?

4b. What further information, if any, does the board need before deciding on this change?

You are now ready for full board discussion and decision.

Chapter 5

Rehearsal Scenarios: The Roles and Responsibilities of Board Members

THIS CHAPTER presents scenarios that deal with the roles of individual board members. Although board members as individuals do not have instructive or evaluative authority over the CEO and staff, they have important responsibilities with regard to the operation and effectiveness of the board itself. Board members who notice that the board is not performing as it said it would, or who wish to clarify the board's rules for itself, or who wish to change a policy of the board have a responsibility to be vocal and active. Likewise, board members have a duty to refrain from undermining board decisions. The scenarios presented in this chapter allow you to rehearse how individuals on the board can use its policies—or those in Resource 3—to constructively contribute their opinions and differences to overall board process.

Rehearsal 5.1

TITLE: Are the Ends Too Broadly Stated?

SCENARIO: An Arts Council board member complains that the Ends policies as written are not sufficiently defined. This particular board member is not willing to accept the full range of reasonable interpretations. What should she do?

Resolve this scenario by answering the following questions:

1. What has the board already said in its relevant policies?

    Ends:

    Executive Limitations:

    Board-Management Delegation:

    Governance Process:

2. According to the board's policies, does this scenario refer to anything that has been delegated to the CEO?

    (*circle*)   Yes   No

    IF YES:

    2a. Does this scenario suggest that the CEO is in compliance with a reasonable interpretation of the board's Ends and Executive Limitations policies?

    (*circle*)   Yes   No   Unsure

    (*Explain your answer.*)

IF NO:

2b. Does this scenario reflect behavior consistent with the board's Governance Process and Board-Management Delegation policies?

(*circle*)   Yes   No   Unsure

(*Explain your answer.*)

3. What action, if any, should the board or board member now take? (*Specify the board or board member actions that you believe would be consistent with governance process and Board-Management Delegation policies.*)

4. If the action you propose involves a possible board policy change:

4a. What amendments or additions do you suggest?

4b. What further information, if any, does the board need before deciding on this change?

You are now ready for full board discussion and decision.

Rehearsal 5.1

TITLE: Are the Ends Too Broadly Stated?

SCENARIO: An Arts Council board member complains that the Ends policies as written are not sufficiently defined. This particular board member is not willing to accept the full range of reasonable interpretations. What should she do?

Resolve this scenario by answering the following questions:

1. What has the board already said in its relevant policies?

   Ends: *Policy 1.0, example F*

   Executive Limitations: *N/A*

   Board-Management Delegation: *The board instructs the CEO through Ends and Executive
   Limitations policies, allowing the CEO to use any reasonable interpretation of these policies
   (3.3). The board will rigorously monitor CEO job performance against Ends and Executive
   Limitations (3.4). In all cases, the board will judge the reasonableness of the CEO's interpretation, as well as whether data confirm its accomplishment (3.4.3). The board is the final
   arbiter of reasonableness (3.4.4).*

   Governance Process: *The board will encourage diversity in viewpoints but emphasize collective, not individual, decisions (4.1). The board will create written governing policies that
   realistically address the broadest levels of all organizational decisions and situations
   (4.2.2). Board members may request that items be placed on the agenda (4.3.2.C). Board
   members will support the legitimacy of the final determination of the board on any particular matter, irrespective of their personal position on the matter (4.5.7).*

2. According to the board's policies, does this scenario refer to anything that has been delegated
   to the CEO?

   (*circle*)   Yes   (No)

   The board, not the CEO, is responsible for writing Ends policies.

   IF YES:

   2a. Does this scenario suggest that the CEO is in compliance with a reasonable interpretation
   of the board's Ends and Executive Limitations policies?

   (*circle*)   Yes   No   Unsure

   (*Explain your answer.*)

IF NO:

2b. Does this scenario reflect behavior consistent with the board's Governance Process and Board-Management Delegation policies?

(*circle*)   Yes   No   (Unsure)

(*Explain your answer.*) *If the board member has presented her concerns to the board, the action was consistent with the board's policy expectations.*

3. What action, if any, should the board or board member now take? (*Specify the board or board member actions that you believe would be consistent with governance process and Board-Management Delegation policies.*) *The concerned board member should request that the item be on the board's agenda and should inform the board of the basis of her concern. She should give an example of a reasonable interpretation that would be unacceptable to her, thus demonstrating her need for greater specificity. If the board agrees with the concern, it should begin to collect options and implications for stating the ends more narrowly, thus reducing the range of interpretation delegated to the CEO. If the board does not share the concern, the board member should be expected to support the legitimacy of the board's decision.*

4. If the action you propose involves a possible board policy change:

4a. What amendments or additions do you suggest? *It may be necessary to define Ends policies more narrowly.*

4b. What further information, if any, does the board need before deciding on this change? *If the board agrees that the policies are insufficiently defined, it should research the options and implications of further policy definition.*

You are now ready for full board discussion and decision.

Rehearsal 5.2

TITLE: Can the CGO Violate Board Policy?

SCENARIO: The CGO approves an expenditure that substantially exceeds the budget for board training established by the board. The board becomes aware of this when the CEO alerts the board to its failure to comply with its own policies. What should the board do?

Resolve this scenario by answering the following questions:

1. What has the board already said in its relevant policies?

   Ends:

   Executive Limitations:

   Board-Management Delegation:

   Governance Process:

2. According to the board's policies, does this scenario refer to anything that has been delegated to the CEO?

   (*circle*)   Yes   No

   IF YES:

   2a. Does this scenario suggest that the CEO is in compliance with a reasonable interpretation of the board's Ends and Executive Limitations policies?

   (*circle*)   Yes   No   Unsure

   (*Explain your answer.*)

IF NO:

2b. Does this scenario reflect behavior consistent with the board's Governance Process and Board-Management Delegation policies?

(*circle*)   Yes   No   Unsure

(*Explain your answer.*)

3. What action, if any, should the board or board member now take? (*Specify the board or board member actions that you believe would be consistent with governance process and Board-Management Delegation policies.*)

4. If the action you propose involves a possible board policy change:

4a. What amendments or additions do you suggest?

4b. What further information, if any, does the board need before deciding on this change?

You are now ready for full board discussion and decision.

REHEARSAL WORKSHEET

Rehearsal 5.2

TITLE: Can the CGO Violate Board Policy?

SCENARIO: The CGO approves an expenditure that substantially exceeds the budget for board training established by the board. The board becomes aware of this when the CEO alerts the board to its failure to comply with its own policies. What should the board do?

Resolve this scenario by answering the following questions:

1. What has the board already said in its relevant policies?

   Ends: *N/A*

   Executive Limitations: *The CEO may not fail to advise the board if, in the CEO's opinion, the board is not in compliance with its own policies on governance process and Board-Management Delegation (2.8.5).*

   Board-Management Delegation: *N/A*

   Governance Process: *The board will allow no officer, individual, or committee to hinder or serve as an excuse for not fulfilling group obligations (4.1.5). The CGO is authorized to make decisions within board policy on governance process and Board-Management Delegation. . . . and is authorized to use any reasonable interpretation of the provisions in these policies (4.4.2). The board allows up to a certain dollar amount for attendance at conferences and workshops (4.8.2.A).*

2. According to the board's policies, does this scenario refer to anything that has been delegated to the CEO?

   (circle)   Yes   (No)

   Although required to inform the board if it does not comply with its own policies, the CEO is not responsible for the fulfillment of the board's own commitments.

   IF YES:

2a. Does this scenario suggest that the CEO is in compliance with a reasonable interpretation of the board's Ends and Executive Limitations policies?

   (circle)   Yes   No   Unsure

   (Explain your answer.)

IF NO:

2b. Does this scenario reflect behavior consistent with the board's Governance Process and Board-Management Delegation policies?

(*circle*)   Yes   (No)   Unsure

(*Explain your answer.*) *The CGO has clearly violated the board's training budget, established in its governance investment policy.*

3. What action, if any, should the board or board member now take? (*Specify the board or board member actions that you believe would be consistent with governance process and Board-Management Delegation policies.*) *As the board is accountable for the actions of its CGO, it should inform the CGO that he or she has exceeded the authority of the position and that this is not acceptable. If the CGO is not willing to use his authority in accordance with the board's delegation to that position, the board, if it has the authority to do so, should consider replacing the CGO with an individual who will respect the board's wishes.*

4. If the action you propose involves a possible board policy change:

4a. What amendments or additions do you suggest? *Unless the board has no authority to replace its CGO, it may choose to add to policy 4.4.2 how it will address noncompliance with the CGO's job requirements.*

4b. What further information, if any, does the board need before deciding on this change? *The board should review provisions in the bylaws pertaining to the authority of the board to remove or replace officers.*

You are now ready for full board discussion and decision.

Rehearsal 5.3

TITLE: What If a Board Member Undermines the Board?

SCENARIO: A board member dislikes the Policy Governance model. He's chosen to disregard the policies and publicly belittles them. What should the board do?

Resolve this scenario by answering the following questions:

1. What has the board already said in its relevant policies?

   Ends:

   Executive Limitations:

   Board-Management Delegation:

   Governance Process:

2. According to the board's policies, does this scenario refer to anything that has been delegated to the CEO?

   (*circle*)   Yes   No

   IF YES:

   2a. Does this scenario suggest that the CEO is in compliance with a reasonable interpretation of the board's Ends and Executive Limitations policies?

   (*circle*)   Yes   No   Unsure

   (*Explain your answer.*)

IF NO:

2b. Does this scenario reflect behavior consistent with the board's Governance Process and Board-Management Delegation policies?

(*circle*)   Yes   No   Unsure

(*Explain your answer.*)

3. What action, if any, should the board or board member now take? (*Specify the board or board member actions that you believe would be consistent with governance process and Board-Management Delegation policies.*)

4. If the action you propose involves a possible board policy change:

4a. What amendments or additions do you suggest?

4b. What further information, if any, does the board need before deciding on this change?

You are now ready for full board discussion and decision.

Rehearsal 5.3

TITLE: What If a Board Member Undermines the Board?

SCENARIO: A board member dislikes the Policy Governance model. He's chosen to disregard the policies and publicly belittles them. What should the board do?

Resolve this scenario by answering the following questions:

1. What has the board already said in its relevant policies?

   Ends: *N/A*

   Executive Limitations: *N/A*

   Board-Management Delegation: *N/A*

   Governance Process: *The board will enforce upon itself whatever discipline is needed to govern with excellence. While the board can change its policies at any time, it will observe those currently in effect (4.1.3). The board will not allow any individual to hinder or serve as an excuse for not fulfilling its obligations (4.1.4). The board will monitor and discuss its performance, comparing board activity and discipline to its policies (4.1.5). The CGO ensures that the board behaves consistently with its own rules (4.4.1). Board members must recognize the inability of any board member to speak for the board, except to repeat board decisions (4.5.3.B). Each member of the board will support the legitimacy and authority of the final determination of the board concerning any particular matter, irrespective of the member's personal position (4.5.7).*

2. According to the board's policies, does this scenario refer to anything that has been delegated to the CEO?

   (*circle*)   Yes

   This scenario is about the actions of the board and its members.

   IF YES:

   2a. Does this scenario suggest that the CEO is in compliance with a reasonable interpretation of the board's Ends and Executive Limitations policies?

   (*circle*)   Yes   No   Unsure

   (*Explain your answer.*)

IF NO:

2b. Does this scenario reflect behavior consistent with the board's Governance Process and Board-Management Delegation policies?

(*circle*)   Yes   (No)   Unsure

(*Explain your answer.*) *The actions of the board member (disregarding and publicly belittling the decisions of the board) are a violation of clearly stated board norms.*

3. What action, if any, should the board or board member now take? (*Specify the board or board member actions that you believe would be consistent with governance process and Board-Management Delegation policies.*) *The board should address the board member, reminding her of its commitment to its policies and to group decisions. The CGO has the authority to see to it that the board does not shirk this responsibility. A board member disagreeing with the board's adopted approach to its job should be invited to present alternatives for board consideration. However, the decision made by the board must be honored. If the board member does not believe she can support a decision made by the board, resignation is an honorable option. For boards with the authority to do so, removal is another option.*

4. If the action you propose involves a possible board policy change:

4a. What amendments or additions do you suggest? *The board may consider amending its governance process policies to reflect steps it will take if a board member violates board policy.*

4b. What further information, if any, does the board need before deciding on this change? *The board should review and ensure that its decisions are consistent with its bylaws. In many cases, bylaws provisions guide what is typically the last resort in board discipline, which is removal of a board member.*

You are now ready for full board discussion and decision.

Rehearsal 5.4

TITLE: Should Board Members with Expertise Oversee Programs?

SCENARIO: A board member has expertise in a program area where the CEO has announced a new initiative. The board member conveys a request to the board that she be given oversight responsibility so that her expertise won't be wasted. How should the board respond to this request?

Resolve this scenario by answering the following questions:

1. What has the board already said in its relevant policies?

   Ends:

   Executive Limitations:

   Board-Management Delegation:

   Governance Process:

2. According to the board's policies, does this scenario refer to anything that has been delegated to the CEO?

   (*circle*)   Yes   No

   IF YES:

   2a. Does this scenario suggest that the CEO is in compliance with a reasonable interpretation of the board's Ends and Executive Limitations policies?

   (*circle*)   Yes   No   Unsure

   (*Explain your answer.*)

IF NO:

2b. Does this scenario reflect behavior consistent with the board's Governance Process and Board-Management Delegation policies?

(*circle*)   Yes   No   Unsure

(*Explain your answer.*)

3. What action, if any, should the board or board member now take? (*Specify the board or board member actions that you believe would be consistent with governance process and Board-Management Delegation policies.*)

4. If the action you propose involves a possible board policy change:

4a. What amendments or additions do you suggest?

4b. What further information, if any, does the board need before deciding on this change?

You are now ready for full board discussion and decision.

Rehearsal 5.4

TITLE: Should Board Members with Expertise Oversee Programs?

SCENARIO: A board member has expertise in a program area where the CEO has announced a new initiative. The board member conveys a request to the board that she be given oversight responsibility so that her expertise won't be wasted. How should the board respond to this request?

Resolve this scenario by answering the following questions:

1. What has the board already said in its relevant policies?

   Ends: *N/A*

   Executive Limitations: *N/A*

   Board-Management Delegation: *Only officially passed motions of the board are binding on the CEO (3.1). Decisions or instructions of individual board members are not binding on the CEO except when the board has authorized such exercise of authority. The CEO is the board's only link to operational achievement and conduct (3.2). As long as the CEO uses any reasonable interpretation of the board's Ends and Executive Limitations policies, the CEO is authorized to establish all further policies, make all decisions, take all actions, establish all practices, and pursue all activities (3.3.3).*

   Governance Process: *The board will not use the expertise of individual members to substitute for the judgment of the board, although the expertise of individual members maybe used to enhance the understanding of the board as a body (4.1.1). There will be orientation of new board members in the board's governance process (4.1.4).*

2. According to the board's policies, does this scenario refer to anything that has been delegated to the CEO?

   (circle)   Yes   (No)

   The scenario addresses not the CEO's actions but those of the board member seeking to oversee them.

   IF YES:

   2a. Does this scenario suggest that the CEO is in compliance with a reasonable interpretation of the board's Ends and Executive Limitations policies?

   (circle)   Yes   No   Unsure

   (Explain your answer.)

IF NO:

2b. Does this scenario reflect behavior consistent with the board's Governance Process and Board-Management Delegation policies?

(*circle*)   ⟨ Yes ⟩   No   Unsure

(*Explain your answer.*) *As the board member brought her request to the board and did not first give directions to the CEO, the board's policies have not been violated.*

3. What action, if any, should the board or board member now take? (*Specify the board or board member actions that you believe would be consistent with governance process and Board-Management Delegation policies.*) *The board should refuse the request for operational responsibility. At the same time, to benefit from its member's expertise, the board should ask the expert board member if she has any worries about possible unacceptable actions or conditions that are not sufficiently covered by existing Executive Limitations policies. This knowledge could help the board strengthen its policies without interfering in the delegation between board and CEO.*

   As the board member is apparently unaware of Policy Governance and how its delegation system assures accountability, the board's orientation process should also be examined.

4. If the action you propose involves a possible board policy change:

   4a. What amendments or additions do you suggest? *If the board member with expertise has concerns that the board feels are both justified and not yet covered sufficiently in policy, the board may find it necessary to amend one or more of its Executive Limitations policies.*

   4b. What further information, if any, does the board need before deciding on this change? *The concerns of the board member with expertise in this operational area should be considered.*

   You are now ready for full board discussion and decision.

Rehearsal 5.5

TITLE: Why Are We Spending So Much Time Talking About This?

SCENARIO: Certain board members are becoming frustrated by the fact that not enough board meeting time is being devoted to ends. What should they do?

Resolve this scenario by answering the following questions:

1. What has the board already said in its relevant policies?

   Ends:

   Executive Limitations:

   Board-Management Delegation:

   Governance Process:

2. According to the board's policies, does this scenario refer to anything that has been delegated to the CEO?

   (*circle*)   Yes   No

   IF YES:

   2a. Does this scenario suggest that the CEO is in compliance with a reasonable interpretation of the board's Ends and Executive Limitations policies?

   (*circle*)   Yes   No   Unsure

   (*Explain your answer.*)

IF NO:

2b. Does this scenario reflect behavior consistent with the board's Governance Process and Board-Management Delegation policies?

(*circle*)   Yes   No   Unsure

(*Explain your answer.*)

3. What action, if any, should the board or board member now take? (*Specify the board or board member actions that you believe would be consistent with governance process and Board-Management Delegation policies.*)

4. If the action you propose involves a possible board policy change:

4a. What amendments or additions do you suggest?

4b. What further information, if any, does the board need before deciding on this change?

You are now ready for full board discussion and decision.

Rehearsal 5.5

TITLE: Why Are We Spending So Much Time Talking About This?

SCENARIO: Certain board members are becoming frustrated by the fact that not enough board meeting time is being devoted to ends. What should they do?

Resolve this scenario by answering the following questions:

1. What has the board already said in its relevant policies?

   Ends: *N/A*

   Executive Limitations: *N/A*

   Board-Management Delegation: *N/A*

   Governance Process: *The board will govern with outward vision rather than internal preoccupation (4.1). The board will cultivate a sense of group responsibility and will be responsible for excellence in governing (4.1.1). The board will emphasize intended long-term impacts outside the staff organization (4.1.2). The board will monitor and discuss its performance at each meeting (4.1.6). The board writes Ends policies (4.2.2.A). The board will complete a reexploration of its Ends policies annually (4.3). The CGO must ensure that the board behaves consistently with its own rules (4.4.1).*

2. According to the board's policies, does this scenario refer to anything that has been delegated to the CEO?

   (*circle*)   Yes   (**No**)

   The CEO is not responsible for the board's agenda content.

   IF YES:

2a. Does this scenario suggest that the CEO is in compliance with a reasonable interpretation of the board's Ends and Executive Limitations policies?

   (*circle*)   Yes   No   Unsure

   (*Explain your answer.*)

IF NO:

2b. Does this scenario reflect behavior consistent with the board's Governance Process and Board-Management Delegation policies?

(*circle*)   Yes   No   (Unsure)

(*Explain your answer.*) *The board's agendas may not reflect its governance commitments.*

3. What action, if any, should the board or board member now take? (*Specify the board or board member actions that you believe would be consistent with governance process and Board-Management Delegation policies.*) *All board members have an obligation to notice whether the board is doing the job it has committed to in its policies. The board should remind itself that all members are accountable for good governance. If insufficient attention is being paid to ends issues, the board should address the apparent failure of the CGO to enforce the board's policies, especially agenda planning. Group responsibility required by the governance process policies would suggest that frustrated board members should voice their frustrations to the CGO and the board. The board should review its agenda planning policy to ascertain if meetings are planned in a manner consistent with this policy. It should consider making more explicit plans for information collection and consideration of Ends policy alternatives.*

4. If the action you propose involves a possible board policy change:

    4a. What amendments or additions do you suggest? *The board may add to the specificity of its plans for meetings by developing a policy that outlines an annual agenda detailing the ends issues about which the board wishes to study or make determinations.*

    4b. What further information, if any, does the board need before deciding on this change?

    You are now ready for full board discussion and decision.

Rehearsal 5.6

TITLE: What If Confidentiality Is Violated?

SCENARIO: A board member discloses confidential information to people not on the board. What should the board do?

Resolve this scenario by answering the following questions:

1. What has the board already said in its relevant policies?

    Ends:

    Executive Limitations:

    Board-Management Delegation:

    Governance Process:

2. According to the board's policies, does this scenario refer to anything that has been delegated to the CEO?

    (*circle*)   Yes   No

    IF YES:

    2a. Does this scenario suggest that the CEO is in compliance with a reasonable interpretation of the board's Ends and Executive Limitations policies?

    (*circle*)   Yes   No   Unsure

    (*Explain your answer.*)

IF NO:

2b. Does this scenario reflect behavior consistent with the board's Governance Process and Board-Management Delegation policies?

(*circle*)   Yes   No   Unsure

(*Explain your answer.*)

3. What action, if any, should the board or board member now take? (*Specify the board or board member actions that you believe would be consistent with governance process and Board-Management Delegation policies.*)

4. If the action you propose involves a possible board policy change:

    4a. What amendments or additions do you suggest?

    4b. What further information, if any, does the board need before deciding on this change?

You are now ready for full board discussion and decision.

Rehearsal 5.6

TITLE: What If Confidentiality Is Violated?

SCENARIO: A board member discloses confidential information to people not on the board. What should the board do?

Resolve this scenario by answering the following questions:

1. What has the board already said in its relevant policies?

    Ends: *N/A*

    Executive Limitations: *N/A*

    Board-Management Delegation: *N/A*

    Governance Process: *The board will enforce upon itself whatever discipline is needed to govern with excellence (4.1.3). The board will allow no officer, individual, or committee of the board to hinder or serve as an excuse for not fulfilling group obligations (4.1.5). The CGO's job is to ensure that the board behaves consistently with its own rules (4.4.1). Members will respect the confidentiality appropriate to issues of a sensitive nature (4.5.4).*

2. According to the board's policies, does this scenario refer to anything that has been delegated to the CEO?

    (*circle*)   Yes   (No)

    The CEO is not responsible for ensuring that board members keep their commitments.

    IF YES:

2a. Does this scenario suggest that the CEO is in compliance with a reasonable interpretation of the board's Ends and Executive Limitations policies?

    (*circle*)   Yes   No   Unsure

    (*Explain your answer.*)

IF NO:

2b. Does this scenario reflect behavior consistent with the board's Governance Process and Board-Management Delegation policies?

(*circle*)   Yes   (No)   Unsure

(*Explain your answer.*) *Respecting confidentiality is a clearly stated expectation of board members.*

3. What action, if any, should the board or board member now take? (*Specify the board or board member actions that you believe would be consistent with governance process and Board-Management Delegation policies.*) *Every board member, especially the CGO, has an obligation to address the problem. The board cannot ignore a breach of confidentiality and must bring to the board member's attention that the behavior is unacceptable. The board should also examine its policy to determine if more policy guidance to board members would be helpful.*

4. If the action you propose involves a possible board policy change:

    4a. What amendments or additions do you suggest? *Further clarification of the issues the board considers to be confidential may be helpful. This would require an amendment to governance process policy 4.5.4. The board may also wish to define the consequences it will enforce if board members breach the confidentiality requirement.*

    4b. What further information, if any, does the board need before deciding on this change? *The board should discuss appropriate steps to be taken when a member of the board team violates board policy. Bylaws provisions regarding corrective actions should be reviewed.*

    You are now ready for full board discussion and decision.

Rehearsal 5.7

TITLE: What If a Dominant Board Member Hijacks the Board?

SCENARIO: A high-prestige board member dominates board deliberations. How should the board respond?

Resolve this scenario by answering the following questions:

1. What has the board already said in its relevant policies?

   Ends:

   Executive Limitations:

   Board-Management Delegation:

   Governance Process:

2. According to the board's policies, does this scenario refer to anything that has been delegated to the CEO?

   (*circle*)   Yes   No

   IF YES:

   2a. Does this scenario suggest that the CEO is in compliance with a reasonable interpretation of the board's Ends and Executive Limitations policies?

   (*circle*)   Yes   No   Unsure

   (*Explain your answer.*)

IF NO:

2b. Does this scenario reflect behavior consistent with the board's Governance Process and Board-Management Delegation policies?

(*circle*)   Yes   No   Unsure

(*Explain your answer.*)

3. What action, if any, should the board or board member now take? (*Specify the board or board member actions that you believe would be consistent with governance process and Board-Management Delegation policies.*)

4. If the action you propose involves a possible board policy change:

4a. What amendments or additions do you suggest?

4b. What further information, if any, does the board need before deciding on this change?

You are now ready for full board discussion and decision.

Rehearsal 5.7

TITLE: What If a Dominant Board Member Hijacks the Board?

SCENARIO: A high-prestige board member dominates board deliberations. How should the board respond?

Resolve this scenario by answering the following questions:

1. What has the board already said in its relevant policies?

    Ends: *N/A*

    Executive Limitations: *N/A*

    Board-Management Delegation: *N/A*

    Governance Process: *The board will govern emphasizing collective rather than individual decisions (4.1) and a sense of group responsibility (4.1.1). The board will not use the expertise of individual members to substitute for the judgment of the board (4.1.1). The board will use whatever discipline is needed to govern with excellence (4.1.3). The board will not let any individual. . . hinder or serve as an excuse for not fulfilling group obligations (4.1.5). The board will monitor itself (4.1.6). The CGO must ensure fair and open deliberations (4.4.1.C). The CGO has authority to rule and recognize (4.4.2.A). Board members must commit themselves to the proper use of authority and appropriate decorum (4.5).*

2. According to the board's policies, does this scenario refer to anything that has been delegated to the CEO?

    (*circle*)   Yes   (No)

    The board itself is responsible for its governance process.

    IF YES:

    2a. Does this scenario suggest that the CEO is in compliance with a reasonable interpretation of the board's Ends and Executive Limitations policies?

    (*circle*)   Yes   No   Unsure

    (*Explain your answer.*)

IF NO:

2b. Does this scenario reflect behavior consistent with the board's Governance Process and Board-Management Delegation policies?

(*circle*)   Yes   (No)   Unsure

(*Explain your answer.*) *The dominant board member has not respected the board's commitments to collective process and decisions. Further, neither the CGO nor the board have exercised the discipline required to ensure an inclusive process.*

3. What action, if any, should the board or board member now take? (*Specify the board or board member actions that you believe would be consistent with governance process and Board-Management Delegation policies.*) *Individual board members dominate board process only if the board allows this to happen.*

If the social awkwardness of dealing with this situation has prevented board members, including the chair, from addressing it individually, the board may need to discuss the importance of giving all members a chance to participate in deliberations. The board may also wish to address the apparent failure of the CGO to use the authority he or she has to rule and recognize in a more inclusive manner. More rigorous board self-evaluation may be helpful in alerting all board members to the need to take responsibility for board process.

4. If the action you propose involves a possible board policy change:

4a. What amendments or additions do you suggest?

4b. What further information, if any, does the board need before deciding on this change?

You are now ready for full board discussion and decision.

Rehearsal 5.8

TITLE: Who's Responsible for New Board Member Orientation?

SCENARIO: The board finds that new board members are unaware of the Policy Governance model and the policies of the board. What should the board do?

Resolve this scenario by answering the following questions:

1. What has the board already said in its relevant policies?

   Ends:

   Executive Limitations:

   Board-Management Delegation:

   Governance Process:

2. According to the board's policies, does this scenario refer to anything that has been delegated to the CEO?

   (*circle*)   Yes   No

   IF YES:

   2a. Does this scenario suggest that the CEO is in compliance with a reasonable interpretation of the board's Ends and Executive Limitations policies?

   (*circle*)   Yes   No   Unsure

   (*Explain your answer.*)

IF NO:

2b. Does this scenario reflect behavior consistent with the board's Governance Process and Board-Management Delegation policies?

(*circle*)   Yes   No   Unsure

(*Explain your answer.*)

3. What action, if any, should the board or board member now take? (*Specify the board or board member actions that you believe would be consistent with governance process and Board-Management Delegation policies.*)

4. If the action you propose involves a possible board policy change:

   4a. What amendments or additions do you suggest?

   4b. What further information, if any, does the board need before deciding on this change?

You are now ready for full board discussion and decision.

REHEARSAL WORKSHEET

Rehearsal 5.8

TITLE: Who's Responsible for New Board Member Orientation?

SCENARIO: The board finds that new board members are unaware of the Policy Governance model and the policies of the board. What should the board do?

Resolve this scenario by answering the following questions:

1. What has the board already said in its relevant policies?

   Ends: *N/A*

   Executive Limitations: *N/A*

   Board-Management Delegation: *N/A*

   Governance Process: *The board will govern lawfully, observing the principles of the Policy Governance model (4.1). The board will enforce upon itself whatever discipline is necessary to govern with excellence (4.1.3). Continual board development will include orientation of new board members in the board's governance process (4.1.4). The board will monitor and discuss its process and performance at each meeting (4.1.6). The board's agenda plan will include governance education (4.3.2.B). The CGO's job is to ensure that the board behaves consistently with its own rules (4.4.1). The board will invest in training to orient new members (4.8.1).*

2. According to the board's policies, does this scenario refer to anything that has been delegated to the CEO?

   (*circle*)　　Yes　(No)

   It is not the CEO's responsibility for new board members to learn their governance job.

   IF YES:

2a. Does this scenario suggest that the CEO is in compliance with a reasonable interpretation of the board's Ends and Executive Limitations policies?

   (*circle*)　　Yes　No　Unsure

   (*Explain your answer.*)

IF NO:

2b. Does this scenario reflect behavior consistent with the board's Governance Process and Board-Management Delegation policies?

(*circle*)   Yes   (No)   Unsure

(*Explain your answer.*) *The board has not fulfilled its commitment to orientation of new board members.*

3. What action, if any, should the board or board member now take? (*Specify the board or board member actions that you believe would be consistent with governance process and Board-Management Delegation policies.*) *Every board member should address the lack of new board member orientation. Since the board has not specified the timing or method of board member orientation, the CGO has the obligation to see that the orientation occurs. The board should expect the CGO to meet this obligation. The board may decide to be more explicit about its expectations for new board member orientation by adding to its policy 4.1.4.*

4. If the action you propose involves a possible board policy change:

4a. What amendments or additions do you suggest? *The board may consider adding to governance process policy 4.1.4 language to the effect that new member orientation should be completed within a specific number of weeks of appointment and should include attendance at a seminar or reading specified texts as well as introduction to the board's policy manual.*

4b. What further information, if any, does the board need before deciding on this change?

You are now ready for full board discussion and decision.

Rehearsal 5.9

TITLE: Should the CGO Withhold Information from the Board?

SCENARIO: The CGO of a trade association learns that the association's new CEO left her former agency (a member of the association) in a financial condition far worse than was known. The CGO is asked by the member agency not to publicize this information, as in its struggle to regain solvency, bad publicity would harm its fundraising efforts. What should the CGO do?

Resolve this scenario by answering the following questions:

1. What has the board already said in its relevant policies?

    Ends:

    Executive Limitations:

    Board-Management Delegation:

    Governance Process:

2. According to the board's policies, does this scenario refer to anything that has been delegated to the CEO?

    (*circle*)   Yes   No

    IF YES:

2a. Does this scenario suggest that the CEO is in compliance with a reasonable interpretation of the board's Ends and Executive Limitations policies?

    (*circle*)   Yes   No   Unsure

    (*Explain your answer.*)

IF NO:

2b. Does this scenario reflect behavior consistent with the board's Governance Process and Board-Management Delegation policies?

(*circle*)   Yes   No   Unsure

(*Explain your answer.*)

3. What action, if any, should the board or board member now take? (*Specify the board or board member actions that you believe would be consistent with governance process and Board-Management Delegation policies.*)

4. If the action you propose involves a possible board policy change:

4a. What amendments or additions do you suggest?

4b. What further information, if any, does the board need before deciding on this change?

You are now ready for full board discussion and decision.

Rehearsal 5.9

TITLE: Should the CGO Withhold Information from the Board?

SCENARIO: The CGO of a trade association learns that the association's new CEO left her former agency (a member of the association) in a financial condition far worse than was known. The CGO is asked by the member agency not to publicize this information, as in its struggle to regain solvency, bad publicity would harm its fundraising efforts. What should the CGO do?

Resolve this scenario by answering the following questions:

1. What has the board already said in its relevant policies?

   Ends: *N/A*

   Executive Limitations: *The CEO will not let the board be uninformed or unaware of significant information such as anticipated media coverage (2.8.4).*

   Board-Management Delegation: *The board will acquire monitoring information by means of internal reports, external reports, or direct board inspections (3.4.2). All policies that instruct the CEO will be monitored at a frequency and by a method chosen by the board (3.4.5).*

   Governance Process: *Acting on behalf of the ownership, the board assures successful performance on Ends and Executive Limitations (4.2.3). The CGO ensures the integrity of the board's process (4.4). The authority of the CGO is to make decisions that are a reasonable interpretation of Board-Management Delegation and Governance Process policies (4.4.2). Board members must be loyal to the ownership, not to staff or other organizations (4.5.1). Board members will respect confidentiality appropriate to issues of a sensitive nature (4.5.4).*

2. According to the board's policies, does this scenario refer to anything that has been delegated to the CEO?

   (*circle*)   Yes   (No)

   There is no evidence of CEO wrongdoing in her current position.

   IF YES:

   2a. Does this scenario suggest that the CEO is in compliance with a reasonable interpretation of the board's Ends and Executive Limitations policies?

      (*circle*)   Yes   No   Unsure

      (*Explain your answer.*)

IF NO:

2b. Does this scenario reflect behavior consistent with the board's Governance Process and Board-Management Delegation policies?

(*circle*)   Yes   No   (Unsure)

(*Explain your answer.*) *The CGO's actions subsequent to learning this information will either be consistent with or violate the board's policies.*

3. What action, if any, should the board or board member now take? (*Specify the board or board member actions that you believe would be consistent with governance process and Board-Management Delegation policies.*) *The CGO has information about the new CEO's past employment record that was not known when the CEO was hired. Although the informant requested that the issue not be disclosed, the board's fidelity to the total membership must supersede that to any individual association member. The CGO's decisions must be consistent with the board's values. The CGO should convey this to the informant and then notify the board of the information learned, with the proviso that board members respect that this is sensitive, confidential information. The board should verify that its methods and frequency of monitoring CEO performance are adequate to ensure confident control over organizational performance.*

4. If the action you propose involves a possible board policy change:

4a. What amendments or additions do you suggest? *The board may deem it appropriate to monitor compliance with fiscal policies more aggressively. This would be done by increasing monitoring frequency and possibly adding external reports or direct inspection monitoring to the monitoring schedule in policy 3.4.*

4b. What further information, if any, does the board need before deciding on this change?

You are now ready for full board discussion and decision.

Rehearsal 5.10

TITLE: If Decisions Have Already Been Made, Why Attend Board Meetings?

SCENARIO: A new board member concerned about an upcoming ends decision mentions to the CGO that she hopes it will get full discussion. The CGO tells her that quite a few board members have discussed this since the last meeting and "the votes have been counted." He encourages her not to raise her concerns, as it would be "disruptive." What should she do?

Resolve this scenario by answering the following questions:

1. What has the board already said in its relevant policies?

   Ends:

   Executive Limitations:

   Board-Management Delegation:

   Governance Process:

2. According to the board's policies, does this scenario refer to anything that has been delegated to the CEO?

   (*circle*)   Yes   No

   IF YES:

   2a. Does this scenario suggest that the CEO is in compliance with a reasonable interpretation of the board's Ends and Executive Limitations policies?

   (*circle*)   Yes   No   Unsure

   (*Explain your answer.*)

IF NO:

2b. Does this scenario reflect behavior consistent with the board's Governance Process and Board-Management Delegation policies?

(*circle*)   Yes   No   Unsure

(*Explain your answer.*)

3. What action, if any, should the board or board member now take? (*Specify the board or board member actions that you believe would be consistent with governance process and Board-Management Delegation policies.*)

4. If the action you propose involves a possible board policy change:

4a. What amendments or additions do you suggest?

4b. What further information, if any, does the board need before deciding on this change?

You are now ready for full board discussion and decision.

Rehearsal 5.10

TITLE: If Decisions Have Already Been Made, Why Attend Board Meetings?

SCENARIO: A new board member concerned about an upcoming ends decision mentions to the CGO that she hopes it will get full discussion. The CGO tells her that quite a few board members have discussed this since the last meeting and "the votes have been counted." He encourages her not to raise her concerns, as it would be "disruptive." What should she do?

Resolve this scenario by answering the following questions:

1. What has the board already said in its relevant policies?

    Ends: *N/A*

    Executive Limitations: *N/A*

    Board-Management Delegation: *Only officially passed motions of the board are binding on the CEO (3.1).*

    Governance Process: *The board will govern with a style that encourages diversity in viewpoints (4.1). A board member may recommend or request an item for board discussion by submitting the item to the CEO no later than five days before the meeting (4.3.2.C). The CGO ensures that deliberation will be fair, open, and thorough (4.4.1.C). The board commits itself and its members to ethical, businesslike, and lawful conduct (4.5).*

2. According to the board's policies, does this scenario refer to anything that has been delegated to the CEO?

    (*circle*)   Yes   No

    The board's decision-making method is not delegated to the CEO.

    IF YES:

2a. Does this scenario suggest that the CEO is in compliance with a reasonable interpretation of the board's Ends and Executive Limitations policies?

    (*circle*)   Yes   No   Unsure

    (*Explain your answer.*)

IF NO:

2b. Does this scenario reflect behavior consistent with the board's Governance Process and Board-Management Delegation policies?

(*circle*)   Yes   (No)   Unsure

(*Explain your answer.*) *The board's actions are not in keeping with its commitments to inclusive process.*

3. What action, if any, should the board or board member now take? (*Specify the board or board member actions that you believe would be consistent with governance process and Board-Management Delegation policies.*) *The board member should convey her concern about the ends issue to be decided and also the impression she has been given that decisions are being made outside of board meetings. She should ask the board if it is serious about the CGO's ensuring a process in keeping with the board's policies. The board should require its members and its CGO to comply with the policy on CGO job and authority.*

   If the board is subject to open-meeting laws, policy 4.5 has addressed the matter of board decision making outside of the board meeting. The CGO is responsible for ensuring that the board meets its legal obligations. If the board is not subject to open-meeting laws, it should consider adding language to policy 4.1 or 4.4 to clarify its commitment to conduct business in an open and inclusive manner.

4. If the action you propose involves a possible board policy change:

   4a. What amendments or additions do you suggest? *The board may decide to be more explicit about committing itself to a fair and inclusive process.*

   4b. What further information, if any, does the board need before deciding on this change? *The board should discuss whether this revision is necessary or if the board's compliance with its existing policies would be sufficient.*

   You are now ready for full board discussion and decision.

Rehearsal 5.11

TITLE: Where Does the Surplus Go?

SCENARIO: During a nonprofit organization's board meeting, a board member expresses concern that there are surplus funds at year-end. How should the board respond?

Resolve this scenario by answering the following questions:

1. What has the board already said in its relevant policies?

    Ends:

    Executive Limitations:

    Board-Management Delegation:

    Governance Process:

2. According to the board's policies, does this scenario refer to anything that has been delegated to the CEO?

    (*circle*)   Yes   No

    IF YES:

    2a. Does this scenario suggest that the CEO is in compliance with a reasonable interpretation of the board's Ends and Executive Limitations policies?

    (*circle*)   Yes   No   Unsure

    (*Explain your answer.*)

IF NO:

2b. Does this scenario reflect behavior consistent with the board's Governance Process and Board-Management Delegation policies?

(*circle*)   Yes   No   Unsure

(*Explain your answer.*)

3. What action, if any, should the board or board member now take? (*Specify the board or board member actions that you believe would be consistent with governance process and Board-Management Delegation policies.*)

4. If the action you propose involves a possible board policy change:

   4a. What amendments or additions do you suggest?

   4b. What further information, if any, does the board need before deciding on this change?

You are now ready for full board discussion and decision.

REHEARSAL WORKSHEET

Rehearsal 5.11

TITLE: Where Does the Surplus Go?

SCENARIO: During a nonprofit organization's board meeting, a board member expresses concern that there are surplus funds at year-end. How should the board respond?

Resolve this scenario by answering the following questions:

1. What has the board already said in its relevant policies?

   Ends: *N/A*

   Executive Limitations: *Financial planning may not fail to be derived from a multiyear plan (2.3). The CEO may not cause or allow development of fiscal jeopardy (2.4), expend more funds than have been received in the fiscal year to date (2.3.1), use long-term reserves (2.4.3), or endanger the organization's ability to accomplish ends (2.6.10).*

   Board-Management Delegation: *The board instructs the CEO through Ends and Executive Limitations policies, allowing the CEO to use any reasonable interpretation of these policies (3.3). The board may change its Ends and Executive Limitations policies (3.3.4). The board will monitor by judging the reasonableness of the CEO's interpretations and whether data demonstrate accomplishment of the interpretation (3.4.3).*

   Governance Process: *The board acts on behalf of the ownership to ensure appropriate organizational performance (4.2). The board creates realistic policies that establish prudent and ethical boundaries within which all operational activity and decisions must take place (4.2.2).*

2. According to the board's policies, does this scenario refer to anything that has been delegated to the CEO?

   (circle)    Yes   No

   The CEO is responsible for management of finances, within the proscribed Executive Limitations policies.

IF YES:

2a. Does this scenario suggest that the CEO is in compliance with a reasonable interpretation of the board's Ends and Executive Limitations policies?

(*circle*) (Yes) No Unsure

(*Explain your answer.*) *A board member is concerned about the organization's reaching the end of its financial year with unspent funds. The CEO is not prohibited from operating with a surplus by any Executive Limitations policy. Maintaining a surplus would likely be seen as a reasonable interpretation of the cited Executive Limitations policies.*

IF NO:

2b. Does this scenario reflect behavior consistent with the board's Governance Process and Board-Management Delegation policies?

(*circle*) Yes No Unsure

(*Explain your answer.*)

3. What action, if any, should the board or board member now take? (*Specify the board or board member actions that you believe would be consistent with governance process and Board-Management Delegation policies.*) *The board will likely answer the board member's question by stating that the surplus is acceptable because it is a reasonable interpretation of existing policy. However, the board should ask the board member if his concern refers to anything not covered by existing board policy. If so, the board may choose to amend its Executive Limitations policies to protect against what it would decide to be an unacceptable condition.*

4. If the action you propose involves a possible board policy change:

4a. What amendments or additions do you suggest? *The financial condition and activities policy (2.4) or the asset protection policy (2.6) may be amended to address the conditions about which the board is concerned.*

4b. What further information, if any, does the board need before deciding on this change?

You are now ready for full board discussion and decision.

Chapter 6

Rehearsal Scenarios: The Board's Job as a Team

THE SCENARIOS presented in this chapter focus on the board's operation as a team in carrying out the governance job. The scenarios involve situations in which the board must *decide* some rules for itself, and ones in which the board must *enforce* its rules upon itself. Your learning in this chapter will be about the board's need to extrapolate from the principles of Policy Governance in making policies that are both consistent with the model and responsive to unique situations. Here you will test your understanding of the principles themselves; you may find it useful to refer to Resource 1 as well as to the policy manual in Resource 3.

REHEARSAL WORKSHEET

Rehearsal 6.1

TITLE: How Much Should Board Members Contribute?

SCENARIO: While policy requires board members to make a token contribution, some board members feel that a more significant financial contribution is an inherent part of nonprofit board participation. Other board members disagree and feel that such a requirement would disqualify persons who would otherwise be effective board members. The issue remains a source of conflict. What should the board do?

Resolve this scenario by answering the following questions:

1. What has the board already said in its relevant policies?

   Ends:

   Executive Limitations:

   Board-Management Delegation:

   Governance Process:

2. According to the board's policies, does this scenario refer to anything that has been delegated to the CEO?

   (*circle*)   Yes   No

   IF YES:

2a. Does this scenario suggest that the CEO is in compliance with a reasonable interpretation of the board's Ends and Executive Limitations policies?

   (*circle*)   Yes   No   Unsure

   (*Explain your answer.*)

IF NO:

2b. Does this scenario reflect behavior consistent with the board's Governance Process and Board-Management Delegation policies?

(*circle*)   Yes   No   Unsure

(*Explain your answer.*)

3. What action, if any, should the board or board member now take? (*Specify the board or board member actions that you believe would be consistent with Governance Process and Board-Management Delegation policies.*)

4. If the action you propose involves a possible board policy change:

4a. What amendments or additions do you suggest?

4b. What further information, if any, does the board need before deciding on this change?

You are now ready for full board discussion and decision.

Rehearsal 6.1

TITLE: How Much Should Board Members Contribute?

SCENARIO: While policy requires board members to make a token contribution, some board members feel that a more significant financial contribution is an inherent part of nonprofit board participation. Other board members disagree and feel that such a requirement would disqualify persons who would otherwise be effective board members. The issue remains a source of conflict. What should the board do?

Resolve this scenario by answering the following questions:

1. What has the board already said in its relevant policies?

   Ends: *N/A*

   Executive Limitations: *N/A*

   Board-Management Delegation: *N/A*

   Governance Process: *The board's purpose is to ensure that the organization "achieves appropriate results for appropriate persons at an appropriate cost" on behalf of owners (4.0). Specific job outputs of the board are those that ensure appropriate organizational performance (4.2). The board creates realistic Governance Process policies stating how the board conceives and carries out its own tasks (4.2.2.C). The board may commit itself to other "job products," such as "donor funding" for which it chooses to hold itself directly responsible (4.2 notation). Board members may request an item for discussion by notifying the CGO (4.3.2.C). Board members will contribute not less than a specific dollar amount each year (4.5.6).*

2. According to the board's policies, does this scenario refer to anything that has been delegated to the CEO?

   (*circle*)   Yes   (No)

   The board itself is responsible for determining the expectations of its members.

   IF YES:

   2a. Does this scenario suggest that the CEO is in compliance with a reasonable interpretation of the board's Ends and Executive Limitations policies?

   (*circle*)   Yes   No   Unsure

   (*Explain your answer.*)

   IF NO:

2b. Does this scenario reflect behavior consistent with the board's Governance Process and Board-Management Delegation policies?

(*circle*)   (Yes)   No   Unsure

(*Explain your answer.*) *There is no indication that current requirements have not been met. The issue addresses whether policy should be changed to require a higher contribution level from individual board members.*

3. What action, if any, should the board or board member now take? (*Specify the board or board member actions that you believe would be consistent with Governance Process and Board-Management Delegation policies.*) *The board members who want the policy changed should inform the CGO of their desire to have this issue as a board discussion item. The board should identify its options and their implications and agree on a process and date by which the board will make a decision.*

4. If the action you propose involves a possible board policy change:

4a. What amendments or additions do you suggest? *The board may amend policy 4.5.6.*

4b. What further information, if any, does the board need before deciding on this change? *Considerations should include impact on board recruitment and potential or likelihood of greater available resources to achieve ends.*

You are now ready for full board discussion and decision.

Rehearsal 6.2

TITLE: Does the Board Job Include Fundraising?

SCENARIO: Although fundraising is required in this organization, it has been delegated to the CEO. Some board members feel that they should be involved in planning and executing fundraising events or campaigns. Other board members feel that they could be helpful to the CEO and staff when fundraising activities take place but do not want to be in charge of fundraising. Still other board members feel that this is a responsibility that should not be part of the board job. What should the board do?

Resolve this scenario by answering the following questions:

1. What has the board already said in its relevant policies?

   Ends:

   Executive Limitations:

   Board-Management Delegation:

   Governance Process:

2. According to the board's policies, does this scenario refer to anything that has been delegated to the CEO?

   (*circle*)   Yes   No

   IF YES:

2a. Does this scenario suggest that the CEO is in compliance with a reasonable interpretation of the board's Ends and Executive Limitations policies?

   (*circle*)   Yes   No   Unsure

   (*Explain your answer.*)

IF NO:

2b. Does this scenario reflect behavior consistent with the board's Governance Process and Board-Management Delegation policies?

(*circle*)   Yes   No   Unsure

(*Explain your answer.*)

3. What action, if any, should the board or board member now take? (*Specify the board or board member actions that you believe would be consistent with Governance Process and Board-Management Delegation policies.*)

4. If the action you propose involves a possible board policy change:

4a. What amendments or additions do you suggest?

4b. What further information, if any, does the board need before deciding on this change?

You are now ready for full board discussion and decision.

Rehearsal 6.2

TITLE: Does the Board Job Include Fundraising?

SCENARIO: Although fundraising is required in this organization, it has been delegated to the CEO. Some board members feel that they should be involved in planning and executing fundraising events or campaigns. Other board members feel that they could be helpful to the CEO and staff when fundraising activities take place but do not want to be in charge of fundraising. Still other board members feel that this is a responsibility that should not be part of the board job. What should the board do?

Resolve this scenario by answering the following questions:

1. What has the board already said in its relevant policies?

   Ends: *N/A*

   Executive Limitations: *N/A*

   Board-Management Delegation: *N/A*

   Governance Process: *The board's purpose is to ensure that the organization "achieves appropriate results for appropriate persons at an appropriate cost" on behalf of owners (4.0). Specific job outputs of the board are those that ensure appropriate organizational performance (4.2). The board creates realistic Governance Process policies stating how the board conceives and carries out its own tasks (4.2.2.C). The board may commit itself to other "job products," such as "donor funding" for which it chooses to hold itself directly responsible (4.2 notation). Board members may request an item for discussion by notifying the CGO (4.3.2.C). Board members will contribute not less than a specific dollar amount each year (4.5.6).*

2. According to the board's policies, does this scenario refer to anything that has been delegated to the CEO?

   (*circle*)   Yes   (No)

   The board must decide its level of responsibility for fundraising.

   IF YES:

2a. Does this scenario suggest that the CEO is in compliance with a reasonable interpretation of the board's Ends and Executive Limitations policies?

   (*circle*)   Yes   No   Unsure

   (*Explain your answer.*)

IF NO:

2b. Does this scenario reflect behavior consistent with the board's Governance Process and Board-Management Delegation policies?

(*circle*)   (Yes)   No   Unsure

(*Explain your answer.*) *The board has made a decision that some of its members would like to revise. This is a legitimate board topic.*

3. What action, if any, should the board or board member now take? (*Specify the board or board member actions that you believe would be consistent with Governance Process and Board-Management Delegation policies.*) *The board must understand that it cannot describe a job as its own and simultaneously hold the CEO accountable for it. If the board wishes to enhance the resources needed for ends achievement by committing itself to a role in fundraising, it should be precise about what exactly it is committing to. If it intends to raise a specific number of dollars per year through, for example, direct solicitation or a gala dinner, it should say so in its board job products policy and understand that the CEO will assume that those funds will become available in his or her financial planning. The CEO will not be accountable for raising those funds. The board must therefore debate and decide if it will raise any funds at all, and if so, what the amount will be.*

4. If the action you propose involves a possible board policy change:

4a. What amendments or additions do you suggest? *The board may amend policy 4.2 to include in its job products an amount that it is committed to procuring for the organization.*

4b. What further information, if any, does the board need before deciding on this change?

You are now ready for full board discussion and decision.

Rehearsal 6.3

TITLE: Results on Whose Behalf?

SCENARIO: In the Association of Independent Hardware Stores, a small group of members specializes in selling electronic goods. This group needs public awareness of its specialty. Members of this group feel that their focus is not sufficiently prominent in the trade association's priorities. They are considering setting up their own organization. What should the board do?

Resolve this scenario by answering the following questions:

1. What has the board already said in its relevant policies?

   Ends:

   Executive Limitations:

   Board-Management Delegation:

   Governance Process:

2. According to the board's policies, does this scenario refer to anything that has been delegated to the CEO?

   (*circle*)   Yes   No

   IF YES:

2a. Does this scenario suggest that the CEO is in compliance with a reasonable interpretation of the board's Ends and Executive Limitations policies?

   (*circle*)   Yes   No   Unsure

   (*Explain your answer.*)

IF NO:

2b. Does this scenario reflect behavior consistent with the board's Governance Process and Board-Management Delegation policies?

(*circle*)   Yes   No   Unsure

(*Explain your answer.*)

3. What action, if any, should the board or board member now take? (*Specify the board or board member actions that you believe would be consistent with Governance Process and Board-Management Delegation policies.*)

4. If the action you propose involves a possible board policy change:

4a. What amendments or additions do you suggest?

4b. What further information, if any, does the board need before deciding on this change?

You are now ready for full board discussion and decision.

Rehearsal 6.3

TITLE: Results on Whose Behalf?

SCENARIO: In the Association of Independent Hardware Stores, a small group of members specializes in selling electronic goods. This group needs public awareness of its specialty. Members of this group feel that their focus is not sufficiently prominent in the trade association's priorities. They are considering setting up their own organization. What should the board do?

Resolve this scenario by answering the following questions:

1. What has the board already said in its relevant policies?

   Ends: *Example E in policy 1.2.A prescribes public awareness as a required result but does not give special focus to members specializing in electronic goods.*

   Executive Limitations: *N/A*

   Board-Management Delegation: *The CEO's accountability is to accomplish any reasonable interpretation of board Ends policies and avoid any reasonable interpretation of board Executive Limitations policies (3.3.3).*

   Governance Process: *The board works on behalf of the owners (members) of the association (4.0). The board's major focus is on intended long-term impacts (4.1.2). The board is to create the link between the owners and the operational organization (4.2.1). The board will reexplore Ends policies annually (4.3). Education related to ends determination will be planned as part of the board's agenda (4.3.2.B). Board members' loyalty to the ownership is to be unconflicted by loyalties to staff, other organizations, or personal interests as consumers (4.5.1).*

2. According to the board's policies, does this scenario refer to anything that has been delegated to the CEO?

   (*circle*)   Yes

   The issue is not about CEO interpretation of Ends policies but about the prioritization of recipients that the board may wish to specify.

   IF YES:

   2a. Does this scenario suggest that the CEO is in compliance with a reasonable interpretation of the board's Ends and Executive Limitations policies?

   (*circle*)   Yes   No   Unsure

   (*Explain your answer.*)

IF NO:

2b. Does this scenario reflect behavior consistent with the board's Governance Process and Board-Management Delegation policies?

(*circle*)   Yes   No   (Unsure)

(*Explain your answer.*) *It is not clear if the board has considered the needs of this segment of the ownership.*

3. What action, if any, should the board or board member now take? (*Specify the board or board member actions that you believe would be consistent with Governance Process and Board-Management Delegation policies.*) *The board must consider if the dissatisfied members have identified a priority that has been unwisely neglected. The board should arrange to hear the concerns of the subgroup and should seek additional information from other interest groups to help it weigh the input received.*

4. If the action you propose involves a possible board policy change:

4a. What amendments or additions do you suggest? *The board may revise its Ends policies (example E) by stating in a new 1.2.A.3 that priority will be given to this group.*

4b. What further information, if any, does the board need before deciding on this change? *The board should identify the pros and cons of elevating this group's needs as a priority. The board must also consider the costs that may result if the subgroup of members leaves and sets up another association. The board must then decide if prioritizing members who specialize in electronic goods is in the best interests of the membership as a whole.*

You are now ready for full board discussion and decision.

Rehearsal 6.4

TITLE: Should Donors Be on the Board?

SCENARIO: A significant funder is threatening to stop contributing to a nonprofit organization unless given a board seat. What should the board do?

Resolve this scenario by answering the following questions:

1. What has the board already said in its relevant policies?

   Ends:

   Executive Limitations:

   Board-Management Delegation:

   Governance Process:

2. According to the board's policies, does this scenario refer to anything that has been delegated to the CEO?

   (*circle*)   Yes   No

   IF YES:

2a. Does this scenario suggest that the CEO is in compliance with a reasonable interpretation of the board's Ends and Executive Limitations policies?

   (*circle*)   Yes   No   Unsure

   (*Explain your answer.*)

IF NO:

2b. Does this scenario reflect behavior consistent with the board's Governance Process and Board-Management Delegation policies?

(*circle*)   Yes   No   Unsure

(*Explain your answer.*)

3. What action, if any, should the board or board member now take? (*Specify the board or board member actions that you believe would be consistent with Governance Process and Board-Management Delegation policies.*)

4. If the action you propose involves a possible board policy change:

4a. What amendments or additions do you suggest?

4b. What further information, if any, does the board need before deciding on this change?

You are now ready for full board discussion and decision.

Rehearsal 6.4

TITLE: Should Donors Be on the Board?

SCENARIO: A significant funder is threatening to stop contributing to a nonprofit organization unless given a board seat. What should the board do?

Resolve this scenario by answering the following questions:

1. What has the board already said in its relevant policies?

   Ends: *N/A*

   Executive Limitations: *N/A*

   Board-Management Delegation: *N/A*

   Governance Process: *The board exists on behalf of the ownership (4.0). Continual board development will include orientation of new board members in the board's Governance Process (4.1.4). The board acts as an informed agent of the ownership (4.2). Board members' loyalty to the ownership must be unconflicted by any personal interest as a consumer (4.5.1).*

2. According to the board's policies, does this scenario refer to anything that has been delegated to the CEO?

   (circle)   Yes   (No)

   The CEO is not responsible for board composition.

   IF YES:

2a. Does this scenario suggest that the CEO is in compliance with a reasonable interpretation of the board's Ends and Executive Limitations policies?

   (circle)   Yes   No   Unsure

   (Explain your answer.)

   IF NO:

2b. Does this scenario reflect behavior consistent with the board's Governance Process and Board-Management Delegation policies?

   (circle)   (Yes)   No   Unsure

   (Explain your answer.) *The scenario concerns decisions about future board composition.*

3. What action, if any, should the board or board member now take? (*Specify the board or board member actions that you believe would be consistent with Governance Process and Board-Management Delegation policies.*) *The funder has already demonstrated strong commitment to the organization's ends. As with all candidates for board membership, he or she should be informed of the board's policies, particularly those that outline the expectations of board members. Chief among these are the requirements that board members must act in the interests of the owners and that no individual board member has authority over the organization. If the individual commits to contributing to the board's governance of the agency by cooperating in the system the board has chosen to use, his or her candidacy should receive due consideration as part of the board's nomination and election process as determined in the bylaws. (Note that whereas funders are owners in for-profit corporations, they are not necessarily owners in nonprofit organizations.)*

4. If the action you propose involves a possible board policy change:

   4a. What amendments or additions do you suggest?

   4b. What further information, if any, does the board need before deciding on this change?

   You are now ready for full board discussion and decision.

Rehearsal 6.5

TITLE: Ownership Linkage: Now What?

SCENARIO: The board's Ownership Linkages Committee has had very positive meetings with an organization representing a segment of the ownership. The committee wants to follow through to ensure that operational ideas suggested in the meeting are implemented. What should the board do?

Resolve this scenario by answering the following questions:

1. What has the board already said in its relevant policies?

   Ends:

   Executive Limitations:

   Board-Management Delegation:

   Governance Process:

2. According to the board's policies, does this scenario refer to anything that has been delegated to the CEO?

   (*circle*)   Yes   No

   IF YES:

2a. Does this scenario suggest that the CEO is in compliance with a reasonable interpretation of the board's Ends and Executive Limitations policies?

   (*circle*)   Yes   No   Unsure

   (*Explain your answer.*)

IF NO:

2b. Does this scenario reflect behavior consistent with the board's Governance Process and Board-Management Delegation policies?

(*circle*)   Yes   No   Unsure

(*Explain your answer.*)

3. What action, if any, should the board or board member now take? (*Specify the board or board member actions that you believe would be consistent with Governance Process and Board-Management Delegation policies.*)

4. If the action you propose involves a possible board policy change:

   4a. What amendments or additions do you suggest?

   4b. What further information, if any, does the board need before deciding on this change?

You are now ready for full board discussion and decision.

Rehearsal 6.5

TITLE: Ownership Linkage: Now What?

SCENARIO: The board's Ownership Linkages Committee has had very positive meetings with an organization representing a segment of the ownership. The committee wants to follow through to ensure that operational ideas suggested in the meeting are implemented. What should the board do?

Resolve this scenario by answering the following questions:

1. What has the board already said in its relevant policies?

Ends: *N/A*

Executive Limitations: *N/A*

Board-Management Delegation: *The board instructs the CEO with written policies prescribing ends and describing situations and actions to be avoided (3.3). From the broadest to more defined levels, the board will develop policies that limit the latitude the CEO may exercise in choosing means. The board will never prescribe organizational means delegated to the CEO (3.3.2). The board may change its policies, thereby shifting the boundary between board and CEO domains (3.3.4).*

Governance Process: *The board's purpose, on behalf of owners, is to ensure that the organization achieves ends and avoids unacceptable actions and situations (4.0). The board's major focus will be on ends, not on the administrative or programmatic means of achieving them (4.1.2). The board will not allow committees to hinder the fulfillment of group obligations (4.1.5). The board is responsible for creating linkage between the ownership and the operating organization (4.2.1). The board creates policies that constrain executive authority by establishing prudence and ethics boundaries for all executive activities and decisions (4.2.2.B). The CGO ensures the integrity of the board's process (4.4). Board committees will reinforce the wholeness of the board's job and never interfere with delegation from board to CEO (4.6). The Ownership Linkages Committee must produce options and implications for board consideration about the ends decisions it will make regarding the needs of disabled persons (4.7.1).*

2. According to the board's policies, does this scenario refer to anything that has been delegated to the CEO?

(*circle*)   Yes   (No)

Board committees are involved with the work of the board, not the work of the CEO.

IF YES:

2a. Does this scenario suggest that the CEO is in compliance with a reasonable interpretation of the board's Ends and Executive Limitations policies?

(*circle*)   Yes   No   Unsure

(*Explain your answer.*)

IF NO:

2b. Does this scenario reflect behavior consistent with the board's Governance Process and Board-Management Delegation policies?

(*circle*)   Yes   (No)   Unsure

(*Explain your answer.*) *As it would act to the detriment of the board's ability to hold the CEO accountable, committee instruction or oversight of operational implementation is inconsistent with the cited policies.*

3. What action, if any, should the board or board member now take? (*Specify the board or board member actions that you believe would be consistent with Governance Process and Board-Management Delegation policies.*) *The board should examine whether it gave the committee instructions that were unclear or misleading. It should clarify that the committee has no operational responsibility and should inform the committee that it has not yet performed the job outlined in policy 4.7.1. The committee should be asked to consider the input it received and extrapolate the ends that the ownership group probably intended the operational suggestions to produce. This "translation" of owner input will enable the committee to give useful feedback to the board. The committee may informally pass to the CEO any operational suggestions it has received, but the committee must remember that it has no instructive authority.*

4. If the action you propose involves a possible board policy change:

4a. What amendments or additions do you suggest?

4b. What further information, if any, does the board need before deciding on this change?

You are now ready for full board discussion and decision.

Rehearsal 6.6

TITLE: How Often Should We Meet?

SCENARIO: Each year, the question of how often to meet arises. Some board members feel the board meets too often, while others value monthly meetings as a means for board members to "keep in touch" with the organization. What should the board do?

Resolve this scenario by answering the following questions:

1. What has the board already said in its relevant policies?

   Ends:

   Executive Limitations:

   Board-Management Delegation:

   Governance Process:

2. According to the board's policies, does this scenario refer to anything that has been delegated to the CEO?

   (*circle*)   Yes   No

   IF YES:

   2a. Does this scenario suggest that the CEO is in compliance with a reasonable interpretation of the board's Ends and Executive Limitations policies?

   (*circle*)   Yes   No   Unsure

   (*Explain your answer.*)

IF NO:

2b. Does this scenario reflect behavior consistent with the board's Governance Process and Board-Management Delegation policies?

(*circle*)   Yes   No   Unsure

(*Explain your answer.*)

3. What action, if any, should the board or board member now take? (*Specify the board or board member actions that you believe would be consistent with Governance Process and Board-Management Delegation policies.*)

4. If the action you propose involves a possible board policy change:

   4a. What amendments or additions do you suggest?

   4b. What further information, if any, does the board need before deciding on this change?

You are now ready for full board discussion and decision.

REHEARSAL WORKSHEET

Rehearsal 6.6

TITLE: How Often Should We Meet?

SCENARIO: Each year, the question of how often to meet arises. Some board members feel the board meets too often, while others value monthly meetings as a means for board members to "keep in touch" with the organization. What should the board do?

Resolve this scenario by answering the following questions:

1. What has the board already said in its relevant policies?

   Ends: *N/A*

   Executive Limitations: *N/A*

   Board-Management Delegation: *N/A*

   Governance Process: *The board will cultivate a sense of group responsibility (4.1.1). The board will enforce upon itself whatever discipline is needed to govern with excellence, including matters such as attendance and preparation for meetings (4.1.3). The board has direct responsibility to create the linkage between the ownership and operating organization, written governing policies, and assurance of successful organizational performance (4.2). The board will follow an annual agenda to complete reexploration of ends annually and improve board performance (4.3). The cycle will start in October with the board's development of its agenda for the next year (4.3.2.B). The CGO ensures the integrity of the board's process (4.4). The board will invest in its governance capacity (4.8).*

2. According to the board's policies, does this scenario refer to anything that has been delegated to the CEO?

   (*circle*)   Yes   (No)

   The board must be in charge of its own job and process.

   IF YES:

2a. Does this scenario suggest that the CEO is in compliance with a reasonable interpretation of the board's Ends and Executive Limitations policies?

   (*circle*)   Yes   No   Unsure

   (*Explain your answer.*)

IF NO:

2b. Does this scenario reflect behavior consistent with the board's Governance Process and Board-Management Delegation policies?

(*circle*)   (Yes)   No   Unsure

(*Explain your answer.*) *It is appropriate for board meeting discussions to address concerns about how the board operates.*

3. What action, if any, should the board or board member now take? (*Specify the board or board member actions that you believe would be consistent with Governance Process and Board-Management Delegation policies.*). *As the primary purpose of board meetings is for the board to do its own work, the board should first agree on what it wishes to accomplish in a given time frame (such as the coming year). The time commitment required should then be addressed. If the time required is more than the board is willing to commit, the board should modify its expectations of itself.*

   The board should distinguish between doing its job and board members' "keeping in touch" with the organization. As the policies don't preclude board members from (nonauthoritative) contact with staff members, those with specific areas of interest may make inquiries without consuming valuable board meeting time.

4. If the action you propose involves a possible board policy change:

   4a. What amendments or additions do you suggest? *The board may wish to amend its agenda planning policy (4.3), perhaps to state the number and schedule of board meetings to take place that year.*

   4b. What further information, if any, does the board need before deciding on this change? *The board should address and discuss its annual agenda. What does the board commit to accomplishing with respect to its "job products" (policy 4.2)?*

   You are now ready for full board discussion and decision.

Rehearsal 6.7

TITLE: Should the Board "Stay Out of the Means"?

SCENARIO: Many board members have concerns about operations, but every time an issue is raised, the "Policy Governance zealots" on the board say, "That's a means issue. We leave such matters to the staff to decide." How should board members respond to this?

Resolve this scenario by answering the following questions:

1. What has the board already said in its relevant policies?

   Ends:

   Executive Limitations:

   Board-Management Delegation:

   Governance Process:

2. According to the board's policies, does this scenario refer to anything that has been delegated to the CEO?

   (*circle*)   Yes   No

   IF YES:

2a. Does this scenario suggest that the CEO is in compliance with a reasonable interpretation of the board's Ends and Executive Limitations policies?

   (*circle*)   Yes   No   Unsure

   (*Explain your answer.*)

IF NO:

2b. Does this scenario reflect behavior consistent with the board's Governance Process and Board-Management Delegation policies?

(*circle*)   Yes   No   Unsure

(*Explain your answer.*)

3. What action, if any, should the board or board member now take? (*Specify the board or board member actions that you believe would be consistent with Governance Process and Board-Management Delegation policies.*)

4. If the action you propose involves a possible board policy change:

4a. What amendments or additions do you suggest?

4b. What further information, if any, does the board need before deciding on this change?

You are now ready for full board discussion and decision.

Rehearsal 6.7

TITLE: Should the Board "Stay Out of the Means"?

SCENARIO: Many board members have concerns about operations, but every time an issue is raised, the "Policy Governance zealots" on the board say, "That's a means issue. We leave such matters to the staff to decide." How should board members respond to this?

Resolve this scenario by answering the following questions:

1. What has the board already said in its relevant policies?

   Ends: *N/A*

   Executive Limitations: *N/A*

   Board-Management Delegation: *The board instructs the CEO with written policies prescribing ends and describing "situations and actions to be avoided." From the broadest to more defined levels, the board will develop policies that limit the latitude the CEO may exercise in choosing means (3.3).*

   Governance Process: *The board's purpose, on behalf of owners, is to ensure that the organization achieves ends and avoids unacceptable actions and situations (4.0). The board's major focus will be on ends, not on the administrative or programmatic means of achieving them (4.1.2). Continual board development will include orientation in the board's Governance Process (4.1.4). The board is responsible for determining policies that place constraints on executive authority by establishing prudence and ethics boundaries for all executive activities and decisions (4.2.2.B). Governance education will be arranged (4.3.2.B).*

2. According to the board's policies, does this scenario refer to anything that has been delegated to the CEO?

   (*circle*)   Yes   (No)

   The manner in which the board controls the organization is for the board to decide.

   IF YES:

2a. Does this scenario suggest that the CEO is in compliance with a reasonable interpretation of the board's Ends and Executive Limitations policies?

   (*circle*)   Yes   No   Unsure

   (*Explain your answer.*)

IF NO:

2b. Does this scenario reflect behavior consistent with the board's Governance Process and Board-Management Delegation policies?

(*circle*)   Yes   (No)   Unsure

(*Explain your answer.*) *The board has not met its commitment to orient its members in its Governance Process. If it had, the concerned board members would recognize that Policy Governance boards do exercise authoritative control over operational means issues, although the method of control is proscriptive, not prescriptive.*

3. What action, if any, should the board or board member now take? (*Specify the board or board member actions that you believe would be consistent with Governance Process and Board-Management Delegation policies.*) *Board members should remind each other that the policies state that the board controls operational means issues by determining boundaries within which the CEO and staff must operate. This reflects the Policy Governance principle to stay out of the means except to state what is unacceptable. The CGO has the responsibility to ensure that the entire board understands that the board has committed to orientation of new members and to engaging in ongoing governance education. The board should identify board members' concerns about operational means and check to see if they are adequately addressed in Executive Limitations policies.*

4. If the action you propose involves a possible board policy change:

4a. What amendments or additions do you suggest? *Amendments should be made to any Executive Limitations policies that the board feels are insufficient.*

4b. What further information, if any, does the board need before deciding on this change?

You are now ready for full board discussion and decision.

REHEARSAL WORKSHEET

Rehearsal 6.8

TITLE: Who Gets the Benefit? Who Doesn't?

SCENARIO: A group advocating on behalf of people with traumatic brain injuries wants the board of the mental health system to include these patients in its Ends policies. How should the board respond?

Resolve this scenario by answering the following questions:

1. What has the board already said in its relevant policies?

   Ends:

   Executive Limitations:

   Board-Management Delegation:

   Governance Process:

2. According to the board's policies, does this scenario refer to anything that has been delegated to the CEO?

   (*circle*)   Yes   No

   IF YES:

   2a. Does this scenario suggest that the CEO is in compliance with a reasonable interpretation of the board's Ends and Executive Limitations policies?

   (*circle*)   Yes   No   Unsure

   (*Explain your answer.*)

IF NO:

2b. Does this scenario reflect behavior consistent with the board's Governance Process and Board-Management Delegation policies?

(*circle*)   Yes   No   Unsure

(*Explain your answer.*)

3. What action, if any, should the board or board member now take? (*Specify the board or board member actions that you believe would be consistent with Governance Process and Board-Management Delegation policies.*)

4. If the action you propose involves a possible board policy change:

4a. What amendments or additions do you suggest?

4b. What further information, if any, does the board need before deciding on this change?

You are now ready for full board discussion and decision.

Rehearsal 6.8

TITLE: Who Gets the Benefit? Who Doesn't?

SCENARIO: A group advocating on behalf of people with traumatic brain injuries wants the board of the mental health system to include these patients in its Ends policies. How should the board respond?

Resolve this scenario by answering the following questions:

1. What has the board already said in its relevant policies?

   Ends: *According to policy 1.0, example D, recipients do not currently include people with traumatic brain injuries.*

   Executive Limitations: *N/A*

   Board-Management Delegation: *The CEO may use any reasonable interpretation of Ends policies (3.3.3).*

   Governance Process: *The board is "an informed agent of the ownership" (4.2). The board is responsible for creation of Ends policies (4.2.2.A).*

2. According to the board's policies, does this scenario refer to anything that has been delegated to the CEO?

   (*circle*) Yes (No)

   The scenario does not address issues delegated for CEO interpretation or action. Rather it addresses a possible revision in the broadest Ends policy (1.0, example D).

   IF YES:

2a. Does this scenario suggest that the CEO is in compliance with a reasonable interpretation of the board's Ends and Executive Limitations policies?

   (*circle*) Yes No Unsure

   (*Explain your answer.*)

IF NO:

2b. Does this scenario reflect behavior consistent with the board's Governance Process and Board-Management Delegation policies?

(*circle*)   Yes   No   (Unsure)

(*Explain your answer.*) *The board's Ends policies do not include the group whose interests are being advanced. It is not clear whether the board has considered the implications of adding people with traumatic brain injuries to the consumers cited in its Ends policies.*

3. What action, if any, should the board or board member now take? (*Specify the board or board member actions that you believe would be consistent with Governance Process and Board-Management Delegation policies.*) *Since the Ends policy cannot be reasonably interpreted to include individuals with traumatic brain injuries, the board may choose to consider the merits and implications of changing its policies to meet the needs of this population. It must request information about not only the cost of including this group but also the impact on other groups, especially those who currently receive the benefits produced by the system. The board must determine what decision information it needs, from whom it needs the information, and how it will proceed with its decision making. It must be aware that in the absence of unlimited resources, it cannot require the system to produce all benefits for all needy people.*

4. If the action you propose involves a possible board policy change:

4a. What amendments or additions do you suggest? *The board may expand the range of recipients to be served by its Ends policies. If this occurs, the board should then define the new Ends policy to the point at which it would find any reasonable CEO interpretation acceptable.*

4b. What further information, if any, does the board need before deciding on this change? *Expanding the existing recipient population will likely affect the organization's ability to serve current clients. The board must decide if this is acceptable. The board may also wish to identify other populations excluded by the Ends policy as written and to decide if this can be justified. Knowledge about available funding as well as the capability of other agencies to serve individuals with traumatic brain injuries would also be helpful.*

You are now ready for full board discussion and decision.

Rehearsal 6.9

TITLE: Who Should Be on the Team?

SCENARIO: A board that recruits its own new board members is wondering what types of people it should look for. How should it answer this question?

Resolve this scenario by answering the following questions:

1. What has the board already said in its relevant policies?

   Ends:

   Executive Limitations:

   Board-Management Delegation:

   Governance Process:

2. According to the board's policies, does this scenario refer to anything that has been delegated to the CEO?

   (*circle*)   Yes   No

   IF YES:

   2a. Does this scenario suggest that the CEO is in compliance with a reasonable interpretation of the board's Ends and Executive Limitations policies?

   (*circle*)   Yes   No   Unsure

   (*Explain your answer.*)

IF NO:

2b. Does this scenario reflect behavior consistent with the board's Governance Process and Board-Management Delegation policies?

(*circle*)   Yes   No   Unsure

(*Explain your answer.*)

3. What action, if any, should the board or board member now take? (*Specify the board or board member actions that you believe would be consistent with Governance Process and Board-Management Delegation policies.*)

4. If the action you propose involves a possible board policy change:

4a. What amendments or additions do you suggest?

4b. What further information, if any, does the board need before deciding on this change?

You are now ready for full board discussion and decision.

Rehearsal 6.9

TITLE: Who Should Be on the Team?

SCENARIO: A board that recruits its own new board members is wondering what types of people it should look for. How should it answer this question?

Resolve this scenario by answering the following questions:

1. What has the board already said in its relevant policies?

   Ends: *N/A*

   Executive Limitations: *N/A*

   Board-Management Delegation: *N/A*

   Governance Process: *The board's purpose is to act on behalf of the ownership to ensure appropriate organizational performance (4.0). The board will use the Policy Governance model, emphasize outward vision, diversity in viewpoints, strategic leadership, collective decision making, and so on (4.1). The board acts as an informed agent of the ownership (4.2). The board may establish annual targets for specific board job product accomplishments (4.2 notation). Board members must be unconflicted by loyalties to staff, other organizations, personal interests as consumers, and the like (4.5). Board members will contribute no less than a specific dollar amount or no fewer than a specific number of hours as operational volunteers each year (4.5.6). The nominating committee will properly screen potential board members (4.7.2).*

2. According to the board's policies, does this scenario refer to anything that has been delegated to the CEO?

   (*circle*)   Yes   (No)

   The board must decide on the skills it requires from itself and its new members.

   IF YES:

2a. Does this scenario suggest that the CEO is in compliance with a reasonable interpretation of the board's Ends and Executive Limitations policies?

   (*circle*)   Yes   No   Unsure

   (*Explain your answer.*)

IF NO:

2b. Does this scenario reflect behavior consistent with the board's Governance Process and Board-Management Delegation policies?

(*circle*)   No   Unsure

(*Explain your answer.*)   *The board is, consistent with its policies, being proactive in addressing its composition needs for the future.*

3. What action, if any, should the board or board member now take? (*Specify the board or board member actions that you believe would be consistent with Governance Process and Board-Management Delegation policies.*)   *The board should contemplate the capabilities, responsibilities, processes, and priorities it has outlined for itself, as noted in the cited policies, and identify people who are able and willing to fulfill these roles.*

4. If the action you propose involves a possible board policy change:

   4a. What amendments or additions do you suggest?   *As the board has delegated responsibility in this area to the Nominating Committee (rather than the CGO), it should consider whether it would accept the full range of reasonable interpretations of "properly screened potential board members." If not, the board may amend its charge to the Nominating Committee (4.7.1) or establish a separate Governance Process policy, stating its expectations about such matters as nominations, qualifications for board membership, and specific composition needs to be addressed in the upcoming nominations process.*

   4b. What further information, if any, does the board need before deciding on this change?

   You are now ready for full board discussion and decision.

Rehearsal 6.10

TITLE: Why Not Tell the CEO What to Do?

SCENARIO: A substantial number of board members, who joined the board subsequent to its adoption of Policy Governance, are uncomfortable with the "negative language" of the Executive Limitations policies. They suggest that from this point forward, the board simply affirm, in positive language, its expectations of the CEO. What should the board do?

Resolve this scenario by answering the following questions:

1. What has the board already said in its relevant policies?

    Ends:

    Executive Limitations:

    Board-Management Delegation:

    Governance Process:

2. According to the board's policies, does this scenario refer to anything that has been delegated to the CEO?

    (*circle*)   Yes   No

    IF YES:

2a. Does this scenario suggest that the CEO is in compliance with a reasonable interpretation of the board's Ends and Executive Limitations policies?

    (*circle*)   Yes   No   Unsure

    (*Explain your answer.*)

IF NO:

2b. Does this scenario reflect behavior consistent with the board's Governance Process and Board-Management Delegation policies?

(*circle*)   Yes   No   Unsure

(*Explain your answer.*)

3. What action, if any, should the board or board member now take? (*Specify the board or board member actions that you believe would be consistent with Governance Process and Board-Management Delegation policies.*)

4. If the action you propose involves a possible board policy change:

    4a. What amendments or additions do you suggest?

    4b. What further information, if any, does the board need before deciding on this change?

You are now ready for full board discussion and decision.

Rehearsal 6.10

TITLE: Why Not Tell the CEO What to Do?

SCENARIO: A substantial number of board members, who joined the board subsequent to its adoption of Policy Governance, are uncomfortable with the "negative language" of the Executive Limitations policies. They suggest that from this point forward, the board simply affirm, in positive language, its expectations of the CEO. What should the board do?

Resolve this scenario by answering the following questions:

1. What has the board already said in its relevant policies?

   Ends: *N/A*

   Executive Limitations: *N/A*

   Board-Management Delegation: *The board will develop policies that limit the latitude the CEO may exercise in choosing the organizational means. The board will never prescribe organizational means delegated to the CEO (3.3.2).*

   Governance Process: *The board will use the Policy Governance model (4.1). Continual board development will include orientation of new board members in the board's Governance Process and periodic board discussion of process improvement (4.1.4). The board will in its Executive Limitations policies establish constraints on executive authority that establish prudence and ethics boundaries within which all executive activity and decisions must take place (4.2.2.B). The board will plan governance education as part of its annual agenda (4.3.2.B).*

2. According to the board's policies, does this scenario refer to anything that has been delegated to the CEO?

   (*circle*)   Yes   (No)

   The board has the right to decide its governance approach.

   IF YES:

2a. Does this scenario suggest that the CEO is in compliance with a reasonable interpretation of the board's Ends and Executive Limitations policies?

   (*circle*)   Yes   No   Unsure

   (*Explain your answer.*)

IF NO:

2b. Does this scenario reflect behavior consistent with the board's Governance Process and Board-Management Delegation policies?

(*circle*)   Yes   (No)   Unsure

(*Explain your answer.*) *The board that does not understand the system it is using has not fulfilled its commitments to board orientation and governance education.*

3. What action, if any, should the board or board member now take? (*Specify the board or board member actions that you believe would be consistent with Governance Process and Board-Management Delegation policies.*) *The board should check to see that board member orientation and education have taken place. If they have not, it must expect the CGO to see to it that they do. Each board member must be capable of explaining the governance system being used, and anyone who is not should conclude that his or her governance education has been neglected. Proscribing means is a way of ensuring control over and accountability for organizational means without unduly restricting the decision-making authority of the CEO. There is no reason to change this basic principle if it is understood.*

4, If the action you propose involves a possible board policy change:

4a. What amendments or additions do you suggest?

4b. What further information, if any, does the board need before deciding on this change?

You are now ready for full board discussion and decision.

Resources

Resource 1

The Policy Governance Model

THE POLICY GOVERNANCE® MODEL is an operating system for boards. Developed by John Carver in the 1970s, it has become known and has influenced governance practice all over the world. Since it offers boards a precision tool for governance accountability, it must be thoroughly understood and carefully used in order for it to deliver on its potential. We provide a brief overview of the model in order to inform or remind the reader of the principles on which it was built and the requirements for process and structure that it imposes on its users. It is not our intention to replace the several more complete explanations of the model (see Resource 4) but more to emphasize the important principles around which the model is built.

The Policy Governance model offers a system that allows boards to address their very weighty responsibilities in a manner that is realistic, practicable, and focused on the most critical organizational issues, those that pertain to the accomplishment of organizational purpose.

It is very common to hear members of traditional boards complain that there is so much to be attended to in their meetings that they never seem to have time to deliberate such matters as the purpose the organization was supposed to serve in the first place. School board members commonly observe that they hardly ever get to discuss the student accomplishments that would justify the use of tax money. Social service and health board members complain that the topic of people getting healthier or more functional never seems to come up in their meetings. Association board members find that they seldom have the chance to ponder the results their members should expect in return for their dues. Corporate board members are commonly overwhelmed by information about corporate activities but spend proportionately much less time considering the return on shareholder investment that they must demand of their company.

It is also common to hear board members admit to being overwhelmed by the number of things that could go wrong in their organizations. Board members are aware that they are accountable for such errors, and it is understandable that they would worry about them. They wonder how they can prevent organizational failures such as activities that are illegal, unethical, or imprudent. Traditionally, they have attempted to prevent disaster by carrying out the tasks themselves. This takes the form of delegating only to a board member or committee or of retaining the right of approval over a management plan. As the history of corporate and nonprofit disasters will attest, this system is not reliably effective. Furthermore, any effectiveness it does have is achieved at a very high price: that of neglecting the importance of accomplishment of purpose and of sacrificing the opportunity to clearly delegate the right to make decisions.

Policy Governance addresses these problems. It allows the board to attend to the important issues of organizational purpose so often left ignored, and it gives the board a method of controlling the organization's activities in a way that is effective yet not unduly intrusive. It answers the many problems we so often hear voiced by board members who attend our workshops, questions about board structure, committees, fiduciary responsibility, and the line between the job of the board and that of the CEO.

Ownership and the Purpose of Governance

Boards exist for one reason only: to ensure on behalf of the organization's owners that the organization performs as it should. The concept of ownership is an important one in Policy Governance. All organizations are owned. The most obvious example is found in corporations, where the shareholders are the owners. But other organizations have owners too. The nature of ownership may not be legally based, but it is useful to view nonprofits as having moral owners. Hence the community is the owner of a community-based organization, and the citizens own city government and school systems as well as state or provincial government.

Owners have the right to determine the purpose of an organization. Consequently, when the board makes decisions that govern an organization, the decisions it makes must be made on behalf of and in consultation with the owners on whose behalf the board serves. The board is, in short, accountable to the ownership.

Boards are accountable to owners for organizational performance. The board, therefore, does not exist for the several counterfeit purposes that an observer would gather from common board practices. The board, for example, does not exist to offer help to the staff, no matter how competently it may think it is able to do so. The board does not exist to fulfill board member needs for involvement; indeed, doing so would damage the independence needed at the board level. The board does not exist to represent all the various constituencies that may claim status as stakeholders; the primary allegiance of boards must be to owners.

The Inevitability of Delegation

Boards must realize that their only purpose is to govern in such a way as to ensure accountable organizational performance, as *they are accountable for the entire organization they govern*. But it is common for boards that do comprehend the true scope of their task to wonder how on earth they can possibly know about and control the entire organization in order to fulfill that accountability. The organization is commonly larger than they can watch or understand and generally employs people who have skills that may be intimidating to board members whose strengths are in other fields.

Boards quickly realize that they are in a position of accountability for more than they can put their hands on and that they must delegate the right to make decisions. Delegation involves giving away authority. Since the board is at the top of the formal organizational chart, the board has all the authority in the organization. No one has authority until the board gives some away. The board's dilemma centers on how to give away authority to make decisions while retaining the accountability for decisions made by others.

The Three Steps to Accountable Delegation

Boards facing both comprehensive accountability for their organization and the need to delegate authority to others understand that parties given authority by the board must be held accountable to the board for the authority they are given. Clarity of delegation is a necessity. The Policy Governance model is designed to allow the board to delegate with great clarity by completing three steps:

1. By expressing the expectations of the job being delegated

2. By assigning the expectations with no ambiguity to the party who is to be held accountable for meeting them

3. By checking that the expectations were met

These steps must be fully completed for the board to know that it has not lost control of organizational performance. The Policy Governance model spells out principles attached to each step.

Before we go into more detail explaining the steps just outlined, we must establish some key principles of board operation.

The One Voice Principle

In Policy Governance, boards take the delegation steps with an understanding of the group nature of their authority. They know that the board has authority but the board members do not. As we often tell our clients, being a member of an eleven-member board does not give its individual members one-eleventh of the board's authority. In fact, board members have no authority; the board as a whole has it all. Therefore, when the board expresses expectations, assigns them, or makes judgments based on checking those expectations, the board's actions can be seen as legitimate; when board members attempt to express expectations, assign them, or make judgments about them, these are simply opinions carrying no authority. It would be impossible for the board's subordinates to differentiate between instructions and opinions without such a principle. Moreover, unless the board holds subordinates strictly accountable for complying with board instructions rather than board member opinions, the subordinates can convincingly justify failing to meet board expectations on the grounds that they were busy following board member opinions.

The one voice principle does not require that board decisions be unanimous; rather it posits that after a fair and inclusive process in which diverse opinions have been aired, the board should make a decision. Some boards recognize as a board decision any motion that garnered the support of a majority of a quorum. Other boards require a higher level of agreement. Policy Governance does not dictate the level of agreement required. It demands only that if the level used by a particular board is reached, all board members must respect the decision and refrain from undermining it.

The Role of Policies

The Policy Governance model requires that the board operate and expect its subordinates to operate according to decisions made by the board. These decisions, which we have referred to previously as expectations, we will now start calling policies. In Policy Governance practice, virtually all board decisions are policy decisions, and all policies are written. They are derived from board values about all organizational and governance issues and differ in conception and appearance from policies developed by boards not using Policy Governance. We will discuss the Policy Governance typology of policies later in this resource. Here we emphasize that all decisions of the board and all decisions that amend previous board decisions must be written. Since the purpose of policies is to ensure that board members and the CEO understand the requirements of their jobs, they must be written so that ongoing reference can be made to them without depending on memory. No one knows accurately what a group said, not even the group itself, unless what it said has been written.

The Role of the CEO

For the purposes of this book, we have assumed that the board has chosen to express its expectations for organizational performance to a chief executive officer, or CEO. Of course, this is not the board's only option, but it is the most common choice of governing boards. The advantage of having made such a choice is that the board is spared the task of dividing labor in the organization between the various persons and departments. The CEO handles the apportioning of components of the board's expectations and is accountable such that his or her choices result in organizational performance that meets board expectations.

We use the term CEO to describe the function of this important job, not its title. The CEO occupies the position on the organization chart just below the board. The CEO is accountable to the board, and the rest of the organization is accountable to the CEO. Hence the board is able to ensure organizational accountability to itself by ensuring CEO accountability to itself. Titles we have seen given to the person in the CEO position include president, executive director, general manager, executive vice president, superintendent, city manager, and many more. The title may be of political importance but does not matter for governance purposes.

Expressing Board Expectations as Policies

The first of the three steps in accountable delegation is, as we noted earlier, that of expressing expectations. Here the board as a body decides the expectations it has of its organization and writes them as policies.

The Policy Governance board, understanding that its accountability is for the entire organization, decides on policies for the entire organization. It uses a classification of policy types unique to Policy Governance in order to ensure that its policies cover all organizational issues. The classification is based on the distinction between ends and means.

Ends

All organizations exist for a purpose. In equity corporations, the purpose is likely related to shareholder value. In nonprofit and governmental organizations, as well as mutual societies, the purpose is to cause some change to occur for people or groups in the world outside the organization. The decisions about change to be made and the persons for whom they are to be made, as well as the priority of the changes to be made, are among the weightiest in the organization. These are ends issues. Boards that do not use Policy Governance barely address these issues at all. Policy Governance boards focus most of their attention on them, for they are the issues whose accomplishment justifies the organization's continued existence. Ends, therefore, directly describe the difference to be made outside the organization, as well as the recipient of the difference. Ends also describe the worth of the difference, expressed commonly as the exchange between resources consumed and benefit created. Clearly, the board's ends accountability is that the organization accomplish board expectations such that the right people or groups get the right results in an amount or at a level that justifies the resources spent.

The board examines the range of ends decisions that it may wish to make and makes those decisions on behalf of the owners of the organization. It formulates Ends policies prescriptively, demanding certain results for certain recipients at certain costs.

Means

For Policy Governance boards, every issue that does not describe a result, a recipient, or the worth or priority of a result—in other words, every issue that is not an ends issue—is a means issue. Clearly, there are many organizational issues that are means issues (because they are not ends issues), and the board is still accountable for them. After all, governance itself is a means issue, and the board is certainly accountable for that! Governance can be seen as a board means issue, one that the board must deal with directly. Its policies about the means of the board outline the rules that the board intends to use about its own job, its relationship with the owners, and the style of delegation it will use. It uses two policy categories to do this: Governance Process deals with a board's definition of its own job, and Board-Management Delegation policies articulate the board's rules about how it will delegate into management and monitor organizational performance.

Most means issues are operational. They include all programmatic decisions, financial practices, personnel conditions, and the entire range of decisions about production, public relations, and so forth.

The board is confronted with a dilemma about how to deal with the means of operations, for it is accountable for these matters and therefore must control them. Traditionally, boards have been encouraged to prescribe operational means, largely through approving staff initiatives. Unfortunately, the practice strongly implies that staff actions that have not been approved are suspect and unauthorized. Further, by approving staff initiatives, boards have found themselves less able to demand accountability. How can they fault staff for decisions, however unfortunate, that they themselves had a hand in making?

Boards have often controlled means prescriptively out of concern for the effectiveness of means. But Policy Governance boards have a much stronger way of ensuring the effectiveness of means: they demand accomplishment of explicitly required ends. Even means that are effective, however, may be a cause for concern. Policy Governance boards are aware that operational means may by their very nature be unacceptable, usually because they are decisions, conditions, or practices that violate standards of law, ethics, or prudence. Accordingly, Policy Governance boards adopt a position regarding operational means that is simple and, for boards, revolutionary. Having demanded organization accomplishment of ends, they authorize operations to use any means that have not been found unacceptable. Boards express their expectations about operational means in policies that do not prescribe those that should be used but instead prohibit some on the basis of their unacceptability. These policies are called Executive Limitations policies. The effect on the organization is galvanizing, as this delegation system has the effect of preauthorizing staff actions and decisions and allowing for reasonable creativity, flexibility, and agility.

Board policies, accordingly, are written prescriptively about ends, prescriptively about board means (Governance Process and Board-Management Delegation), and proscriptively about operational means (Executive Limitations).

The Problem of Interpretation

Since the board must make policy for the entire organization, it follows that its policies must be very broad, as policies that address part of the organization would not serve the purpose of establishing control over all of it. Expressing board values or expectations about ends, board means, or operational means in policies formulated broadly serves the purpose of being inclusive. However, an obvious drawback to broad inclusive policies is that such policies are open to a wide range of interpretation. Of course, all policies, since they contain words, are open to interpretation, so the board can never completely avoid expressing its expectations in a manner that someone else must interpret. The board can, however, limit the range of interpretation it delegates.

Policy Governance boards use a system for organizing their policies in the categories described so that they can limit the range of interpretation they allow to a delegatee. The system is based on the fact that values come in sizes. Policies can be broad, open to a wide range of interpretation, or they can be narrow, open to a smaller range of interpretation. An example of a broad Ends policy might be "People with developmental disabilities will have the ability to use their time productively and enjoyably," whereas a narrower version of the same topic could be "Julie will learn to clean her room and play cooperatively with her roommates." An example of a broad board means policy might be "This board will connect governance and management through the use of a single CEO titled 'Executive Director,'" while a narrower version of the same type could be "In order to maintain CEO accountability to the board, no instructions will be given to any other party in management except the CEO." An example of a broad operational means policy might be "The CEO shall not cause or allow any condition, decision, practice, activity, or organizational circumstance that is illegal, imprudent, or unethical," while a more narrowly defined policy in the same category could read "The CEO shall not cause or allow the current ratio to drop below 1.3:1."

Values of various sizes can be nested together, much as mixing bowls of various sizes nest together (see Figure 1). Direct control of the outside items in a nested set of bowls—or the larger items in a nested set of values—allows the inside elements to be both under control and flexible. Direct control can be extended to reduce the range of indirect control (see Figure 2).

The Policy Governance board views each of its policy categories as nested sets. It defines its policy at the broadest level in each category and further defines its policies, moving deeper into the set until it has defined its words sufficiently to delegate them. The board recognizes the point of delegation when it has reached a level of specificity that allows it to agree that it will accept *any reasonable interpretation* of its policy. The board must be aware that it cannot expect its delegatee to make the interpretation of policy that the board members hoped for or that the board members meant. The delegatee is authorized to interpret what the board *said* and must be supported if he or she chose any of the range of interpretations that can be shown to be reasonable.

FIGURE 1

A Nested Set

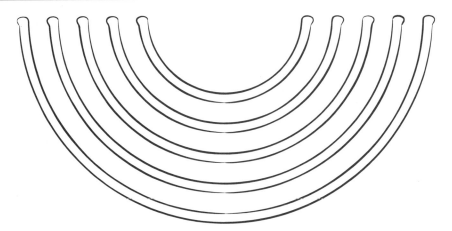

Note: Smaller issues fit within larger issues as smaller bowls fit within larger ones. The entire set can be controlled by handling only the outermost bowl.

FIGURE 2

Hands-On and Hands-Off Control

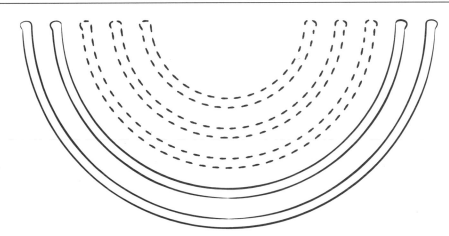

Note: Direct control of the outer bowls in a nested set allows indirect control of the smaller bowls. A board might decide to have hands-on control over the very largest issues (depicted here by bowls drawn with a solid line) but indirect or hands-off control of smaller issues (depicted by bowls drawn with a broken line).

The four categories of board policy, arranged as nested sets, are set out in Figure 3. The circle represents the entire organization, and this figure shows that it has been separated into ends and means, with means being further separated into board means (Governance Process and Board-Management Delegation) and operational or staff means.

Figure 4 shows the policy circle with board policies in each quadrant. It also shows that inside board policy in each quadrant is the area delegated to others to decide. On the left side of the circle is the area in which the chief governance officer (CGO) has authority to interpret board policy and see to it that it is carried out. The CGO is the board officer more commonly referred to as the chair but whose function is considerably more extensive than chairing board meetings. On the right of the circle, the CEO has the authority to interpret and carry out board Ends policy within the boundaries established in Executive Limitations policies.

FIGURE 3

The Policy Circle

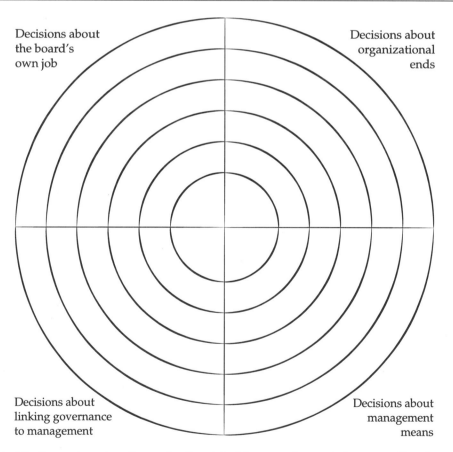

Note: The four categories of organizational decisions are shown as four sets of bowls, brought together to form four quadrants of a circle. Larger and smaller issues within those categories are shown as larger and smaller bowls.

FIGURE 4

Board Policymaking

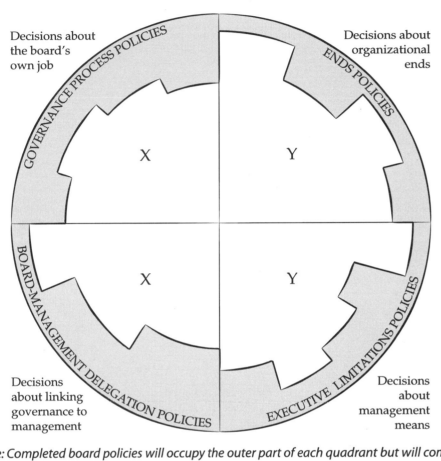

Note: Completed board policies will occupy the outer part of each quadrant but will come into more detail (smaller-bowl levels), the amount depending on the board's values. The board will go into more detail about some policy topics than others, even within a given quadrant. Notice that the quadrant containing all staff means issues will be addressed by the board in a constraining or negative fashion, hence the policy category titled "Executive Limitations." Empty space in the middle represents smaller decisions the board is content to leave to delegatees. The CGO will be given authority to make decisions in the spaces marked X. The CEO will be given authority to make decisions in the spaces marked Y.

Setting the board's expectations for the Policy Governance board therefore involves defining required ends, prohibited operational means, and required board means. In every case, these policies are written first very broadly and then refined in progressively greater levels of detail until the board agrees that it can accept any reasonable interpretation from its delegatee.

Examples of policies that conform to these principles are shown in Resource 3.

Assigning the Board's Expectations

As we have said, to accomplish the first step in accountable delegation, the board must state its expectations of the job being delegated. To accomplish the second of the three steps, the board must assign its expectations to the party who will be held accountable to the board for meeting those expectations. Since the board wishes to retain control of the delegated job, it is crucial that the board be very clear about who is to receive the delegation.

The Policy Governance board, as we have noted, spells out its expectations for its own performance and conduct in documents called Governance Process and Board-Management Delegation policies. The board assigns to its chief governance officer the job of helping the board carry out its governance in accordance with these policies. Hence the CGO is given authority by the board that can be exercised over the board. This authority is held for the purpose of ensuring that the board does the job it said it would do. Because leaderless groups are seldom models of effectiveness or efficiency, the role of CGO is very important. The CGO commonly chairs the board meetings, though the role is more far-reaching than this. The CGO is also responsible for seeing that the board's agenda conforms to the board's expectations for its job, that the orientation and self-evaluation required by the board are carried out, and that the board observes its own rules when making decisions and judgments. In Figure 4, the CGO is shown on the left side of the circle. You will notice that the authority of the CGO is not seen on the right side of the circle. Hence the authority of the CGO does not extend to making decisions or interpretations on the right side of the policy circle, about ends and operational means. This arrangement clearly indicates that it is the board and its CGO who are responsible that the board governs, not the CEO. Although some of the administrative logistics of governance likely would be left to staff, relying on the CEO to take the lead would amount to an admission that the board is unable to manage its own job.

The Policy Governance board spells out its expectations for organizational performance in documents called Ends and Executive Limitations policies. It assigns to the CEO the right to make the interpretations and decisions regarding these board policies. In Figure 4, this assignment is shown with the CEO being placed on the right side of the circle. This is in keeping with the board's choice to use the CEO position as one that is accountable to the board for organizational performance. Organizational performance, led by the CEO, must meet the board's expectations as expressed in policy. Accordingly, the board must be careful to assign those expectations only to the CEO, for to doubly delegate expectations would cause the accountability link between board and CEO to be seriously weakened if not severed.

Traditionally, boards have found a number of ways to blur the accountability of the CEO and the assignment of expectations to this officer. Policy Governance boards avoid doing this. If a function falls within the CEO's delegated area, the board is careful not to assign responsibility for that function to a committee or an officer as that would be to delegate the responsibility twice. As a result, Policy Governance boards tend to have far fewer committees than their more traditional counterparts. Personnel, program, public relations, finance, and similar operational committees are not relevant to Policy Governance boards because their purpose is to be involved in matters for which the CEO is accountable. Boards have committees only if they decide that they need help with their own job, never because they want to help with or advise on CEO responsibilities.

For the same reason, Policy Governance boards either have no treasurer on the board or will use this officer to advise the board, not the staff.

Checking That Expectations Were Met

The third step in accountable delegation involves assessing if the performance expectations delegated by the board were met. It is clear that this step cannot be completed in the absence of written expectations. Checking, evaluating, monitoring, appraising—these are necessarily acts of comparison. What actually resulted must be compared to what the board expected.

Policy Governance boards must approach this step of their job with great rigor. They have defined expectations and allowed their delegatees to use any reasonable interpretation in carry out their jobs. It is important, therefore, that boards assess the reasonableness of the interpretations made as well as task accomplishment.

When the board assesses its own performance and that of its CGO, it must compare what it actually did to what it said it expected. If the board has a policy stating that it will focus mainly on deciding the long-term ends of the organization rather than the programmatic means of achieving them, evaluation must consist of the board's examining whether it lived up to this and whether the CGO assisted in this resolve. This is board self-evaluation.

The board must of course monitor organizational performance and hold the CEO accountable for the results. To do this with rigor, the board must demand information that discloses the interpretations made by the CEO so that a judgment can be made of the reasonableness of the interpretations. It must also demand data that demonstrate the degree of accomplishment of the task as interpreted. These data can be obtained from the CEO or from sources under CEO authority (the internal report), from sources outside the organization, and directly hired by the board (the external report); in rare instances, the board can obtain the data itself. The board must determine the frequency with which it will require monitoring with respect to each of its policies, the schedule being a matter of Board-Management Delegation. Monitoring in this way will allow the board to produce optimally objective judgments regarding CEO compliance with board policies.

Having judged performance and found it to be consistent with expectations, the board may still wish to change its expectations, thus demanding a change in future organizational performance.

Alternatively, the board may judge performance to be inconsistent with a reasonable interpretation of its policies. In this case, the board may consider whether its policies themselves were the problem and change them if they were. The board may, however, find that its policies demanded performance that the board regards as both practicable and desirable, and yet the policies were not followed. The appropriate board response in this case is not to help the CEO fix the problem but rather to decide, with CEO input, about when the problem will be fixed and remonitor at that time. Where there is significant failure to meet the board's policy expectations, the board has discovered that its CEO may not be able to lead the organization to the performance desired by the board.

Decisions to replace a CEO are serious and will not be made lightly; a board must use its judgment in weighing the relative merits of either exercising patience to allow system improvements or taking steps to find a CEO who can more reliably lead the organization to success as defined by the board.

The Board's Own Job

Policy Governance describes the job of the board as three products or outputs. Note that it is not necessary to describe what the board stays busy doing as long as it is clear what any legitimate activity is to produce. The three job products are as follows:

- A linkage between the owners and the operators
- Written governing policies (about Ends, Executive Limitations, Board-Management Delegation, and Governance Process)
- The assurance of organizational performance (If the board has chosen to use a CEO position, this is synonymous with CEO performance.)

The Policy Governance board knows that it holds its authority on behalf of the organization's owners. When it establishes its expectations for organizational performance, it does so on behalf of the owners, and hence it needs to spend some time researching the undoubtedly diverse views of owners with respect to organizational purpose. In addition to owner input, the board must seek whatever expert advice will help it make wise decisions. Its first job product, therefore, is an informed voice of the owners in the governance of the organization.

The Policy Governance board's second job product is the written governing policies with respect to Ends, Executive Limitations, Governance Process, and Board-Management Delegation. Ends policies, written from a long-term perspective, are the most difficult, and although they are usually quite brief, they take the most time of all the policy work of the board. This is understandable, as these policies deal with organizational purpose.

The final job product of the governing board is the assurance that organization function is consistent with board policies, that is, that any reasonable interpretations of ends are accomplished and that any reasonable interpretations of the board's limits on operational means are avoided. The board will need to attend to the hiring, remuneration, monitoring, and if necessary, replacement of the CEO to accomplish this product.

Externally Imposed Requirements

Many Policy Governance boards find that they wish to delegate decision-making authority to the CEO but are required by law, funders, or accreditors to make certain decisions themselves. For example, it is not uncommon for some boards to be required by funders to approve budgets or by regulators to approve staff hires. In these circumstances, Policy Governance boards should remember that they have policies that describe what decisions they would find unacceptable in relation to these topics. The board should require that the CEO bring to the board for approval all matters that the board is compelled to approve, along with a monitoring report that demonstrates that no unacceptable decisions have been made. These items go on the consent agenda. As long as the board finds the monitoring report to demonstrate compliance with the applicable policy, the consent agenda can be dealt with in a rapid vote of acceptance.

The Board's Nongovernance Tasks

In some instances, a board will decide to take on nongovernance tasks in addition to its core job. Examples include boards that commit themselves to producing funds or that decide to undertake regulatory changes or regulator awareness. It is important that these boards understand that retaining these responsibilities for themselves means that the CEO has no accountability for them. Further, it is important that they describe exactly what their additional contributions are to be. The board that is committed to raising $5,000 out of a revenue base of hundreds of thousands or even millions of dollars should avoid stating that it will accept responsibility for all fundraising. Clarity about the role the board commits to makes it possible for the CEO to recognize his or her responsibility for the remainder.

The Benefits of Governing the Policy Governance Way

Although Policy Governance is a more demanding system than many boards have attempted, the benefits of using it are numerous.

First, boards can focus on the future. Policy Governance boards are able to focus on the future results their organization should accomplish, as well as the worth and the recipients of those results (Ends). It is hard for a board to do this if it also has to attend to decisions about more current operational issues, such as purchases, budgets, staffing problems, or public relations.

Second, boards can be in meaningful control of their organizations, even if they are very large and complex, without meddling in them. Policy Governance boards control their organizations by deciding the broader issues about both ends and means, thereby allowing others to decide smaller issues.

Third, boards can delegate meaningful authority to others without failing in their own accountabilities. Policy Governance boards find that it takes a strong board to enable strong leadership at subordinate levels. The parameters of delegated authority are clearly established by the board, allowing decisive leadership by others.

Fourth, boards can evaluate their organization's performance. Policy Governance boards know what they are looking for when they check on organizational performance. Clearly established criteria, contained in policies, increase the probability of organizational compliance with board expectations. Simply put, the board is more likely to get what it wants if it says what it wants.

Fifth, the board and its members know what is required of them. Policy Governance boards have clearly articulated their expectations of the board, its members and CGO, and its committees. Since the design of the board's job has already been decided, the board can distinguish its proper course of action when confronted by questions, without having to spend time defining the nature of governance itself.

Sixth, participation on a Policy Governance board allows board members to experience that they can make a difference.

The Challenge of Governing the Policy Governance Way

Policy Governance is a system that prescribes board behaviors that differ from the traditional practice of boards. It is unsurprising that boards new to governing the Policy Governance way find it challenging and sometimes perplexing when confronted by situations and decisions.

In virtually every case, the answer to the perplexity can be found by a deliberative process that begins with a simple question: "What has the board already said about this in its relevant policies?" The policies established by the board and housed in the policy manual, because they are formulated broadly, will have, at some level, addressed the problem confronting the board. Referring to the existing policies and either following them or changing them in a model-consistent manner is the most useful method for a board to use to solve the many questions it faces. Such a process will establish if the issue is a board issue at all or one in the area delegated to the CEO. It will allow the board to review the policies that the CEO must use in his or her decision making, altering them if this is indicated. It will help a board decide how to react to information that seems to be evaluative but about which the board has stated no criteria, and it will assist the board in reviewing the expectations that it has set for itself and ensuring that it carries out its own job consistent with its own commitments.

For additional and more detailed information about the Policy Governance model, refer to the works listed in Resource 4.

Resource 2
Rehearsal Worksheet

IN THIS RESOURCE you will find a blank copy of the worksheet that we have developed to guide you through rehearsals. Make copies of this worksheet if you wish. Copies can also be printed from the CD-ROM that accompanies this book.

TITLE:

SCENARIO:

Resolve this scenario by answering the following questions:

    1. What has the board already said in its relevant policies?

    Ends:

    Executive Limitations:

    Board-Management Delegation:

    Governance Process:

    2. According to the board's policies, does this scenario refer to anything that has been delegated to the CEO?

    (*circle*)   Yes   No

    IF YES:

    2a. Does this scenario suggest that the CEO is in compliance with a reasonable interpretation of the board's Ends and Executive Limitations policies?

        (*circle*)   Yes   No   Unsure

        (*Explain your answer.*)

IF NO:

2b. Does this scenario reflect behavior consistent with the board's Governance Process and Board-Management Delegation policies?

(*circle*)   Yes   No   Unsure

(*Explain your answer.*)

3. What action, if any, should the board or board member now take? (*Specify the board or board member actions that you believe would be consistent with governance process and board-management delegation policies.*)

4. If the action you propose involves a possible board policy change:

4a. What amendments or additions do you suggest?

4b. What further information, if any, does the board need before deciding on this change?

You are now ready for full board discussion and decision.

Resource 3

A Sample Board Policy Manual

IN THE FOLLOWING PAGES we present a sample board policy manual. Consistent with the principles of the Policy Governance model (explained in greater detail in Resource 1), this manual contains policies in the Governance Process, Board-Management Delegation, Ends, and Executive Limitations categories.

These policy samples were initially developed by John Carver and have been amended by John and Miriam Carver over several years. We have made some additional modifications to them. They are presented here in the format typically used by Policy Governance boards. They demonstrate one of Policy Governance's greatest strengths: its use enables a board to address, at the broadest levels, all organizational circumstances.

Board-Management Delegation policies (Section 3) embody principles about the connection between governance and management that are employed by all Policy Governance boards that use a CEO function. *Governance Process* policies (Section 4) describe basic principles about the board's job, its relationship to owners, its use of officers and committees, and specific expectations of how a board will carry out its work. Policies in these two sections are very similar across the variety of boards using Policy Governance. Since boards tend to share common values regarding the operational means they would deem unacceptable, *Executive Limitations* policies (Section 2) also do not differ greatly among Policy Governance boards. This is why these samples have been demonstrated to have very broad applicability.

Every organization is unique. But from a policy point of view, that uniqueness lies predominantly in ends, not in means. Consequently, no specific *Ends* policy (Section 1) is applicable across organizations, even those of the same type. This is why we've provided Ends policy samples for different types of organizations. We've included examples of Ends policies for a school system, a credit union, an arts organization, a mental health authority, a trade association, and a for-profit corporation.

Completing the rehearsal scenarios and worksheets in this book requires that you refer to board policies. Readers who serve on a Policy Governance board (a board using fully developed policies in these four categories) should refer to their policy manuals. Those whose boards have not yet put their "playbooks" into place will find this sample manual to be a convenient resource. Of course, even those with their own manuals may find it interesting to compare our wording to theirs, and we encourage this use of our samples as well.

Let us stress, however, that the policies that follow are samples only. While the principles articulated in the Governance Process, Board-Management Delegation, and Executive Limitations policies are integral to the systematic accountability that Policy Governance offers, the specific wording and the level of specificity of the policies adopted should be a conscious choice made by a particular board.

The completed worksheets in Chapters Three through Six use the wording and reference numbers of the policies in this resource. To be able to understand and critique our answers, you will need to refer to this manual.

Here is a registry of the policies in this manual:

Ends

1.0. Example A (credit union Ends policies)

1.0. Example B (for-profit corporate Ends policies)

1.0. Example C (school system Ends policies)

1.0. Example D (mental health system Ends policies)

1.0. Example E (trade association Ends policies)

1.0. Example F (arts council Ends policies)

Executive Limitations

2.0. Global Executive Constraint

2.1. Treatment of Consumers

2.2. Treatment of Staff

2.3. Financial Condition and Activities

2.4. Financial Planning and Budgeting

2.5. Emergency CEO Succession

2.6. Asset Protection

2.7. Compensation and Benefits

2.8. Communication and Support to the Board

Board-Management Delegation

3.0. Global Governance-Management Connection

3.1. Unity of Control

3.2. Accountability of the CEO

3.3. Delegation to the CEO

3.4. Monitoring CEO Performance

Governance Process

4.0. Global Governance Commitment

4.1. Governing Style

4.2. Board Job Products

4.3. Agenda Planning

4.4. Chief Governance Officer's Role

4.5. Board Members' Code of Conduct

4.6. Board Committee Principles

4.7. Board Committee Structure

4.8. Governance Investment

Policy Type: Ends
Policy Title: 1.0. Example A (Credit Union Ends Policies)

1. The Credit Union exists for the financial self-sufficiency of its members.

2.A. Members will have the ability to transact personal business on a 24/7 basis.

    2.A.1. Members will be able to make deposits, withdrawals, transfers, and payments at times of their choosing.

    2.A.2. Costs to members will be the actual costs of this result, except where preferential pricing is applied to encourage customer loyalty.

2.B. Members who are able to repay loans will be able to obtain credit at a competitive cost.

    2.B.1. Loans will be available for primary residences, education, and vehicles, with the exception of recreational vehicles.

    2.B.2. Credit will be available for all members over the age of eighteen.

2.C. Members will receive a competitive return on their funds.

    2.C.1. Members' savings will yield interest at a rate better than competitively available.

2.C.1.a. Savings of minor members will yield a higher rate than that available to other members.

2.D. Members will have the information that will assist them in wise financial decision making.

2.D.1. Members will be able to obtain sound plans for their retirement.

2.D.2. Members will have the knowledge they need to decide their insurance needs.

2.D.3. Members will be aware of the risks and benefits of a variety of investment options.

Policy Type: Ends
Policy Title: 1.0. Example B (For-Profit Corporate Ends Policies)

1. The ultimate aim of the company is return on shareholder equity better than the return for firms of similar risk characteristics.

2. Risk characteristics for comparison will include similar size, industry, and maturity of market.

3. Better return will mean above the median of such firms, rather than above the average.

Policy Type: Ends
Policy Title: 1.0. Example C (School System Ends Policies)

1. The school system exists so that young people have the knowledge and abilities needed to prepare them for the next stage of their lives and that justify the expenditure of available funds.

2.A. The first priority is that students will be academically ready to progress.

2.A.1. Students will have the numeracy and literacy skills that reflect their utmost potential.

2.A.2. Students will understand art, science, and technology at a level that prepares them for a complex world.

2.A.3. Students who are academically gifted, if they desire to do so, will secure admission to four-year postsecondary education.

2.A.4. Students entering grade one will be ready to learn.

2.B. The second priority is that students will have an understanding of the world in which they live as well as experience in contributing to it.

2.B.1. Students will have an understanding of world history and geography.

2.B.2. Students will be knowledgeable about the world's major political and religious ideologies.

2.B.3. Students will participate in nonschool community activities that reflect their understanding of citizenship.

2.C. The third priority is that students will have the social skills to be successful in groups of increasing complexity.

2.C.1. Students will be able to share, negotiate solutions to problems, respect diversity, and act assertively.

2.C.2. Students will have knowledge of factors that should guide their decision making about drug use and sexuality.

2.C.3. Students will be capable of making decisions in and for groups.

Policy Type: Ends
Policy Title: 1.0. Example D (Mental Health System Ends Policies)

1. The mental health system exists so that people with mental health challenges, substance abuse problems, and developmental disabilities, as well as affected families, will function at their highest potential in an accepting community, to an extent that justifies the expenditure of available funds.

2.A. The highest priority, where the total need must be met, is that persons in life-disrupting crises will resume functioning at their precrisis equilibrium.

2.A.1. Families affected by crises will be able to function and make decisions in their interests as well as in the interests of the patient.

2.A.2. Patients will learn methods of coping with the challenges that cause crises.

2.A.2.a. Patients will learn to manage their addictions.

2.A.2.b. Patients will be aware of the consequences of decisions they make about the use of prescribed medication.

2.B. Sharing the second priority, chronically affected patients will learn what they need to know to cope with their condition and lead lives that are active and fulfilling.

2.B.1. Skills in activities of daily living and social skills will allow patients to participate to the level of their ability.

2.B.1.a. Patients will have jobs or an alternative way of productively using their time.

2.B.2. Families will be able to discern the needs of their members for support.

2.C. Sharing the second priority, people experiencing transitional mental health issues will gain the understanding and skill they need to resolve problems and maintain functioning.

2.C.1. Patients will be able to solve interpersonal problems without violence.

2.C.2. Parents will have the ability to raise and discipline their children constructively.

2.D. The third priority is that the community will be understanding of the problems associated with substance abuse, developmental disabilities, and disruptions to mental health.

2.D.1. People with mental health challenges or developmental disabilities will be welcomed in neighborhoods, churches, stores, and public facilities.

Policy Type: Ends
Policy Title: 1.0. Example E (Trade Association Ends Policies)

1. The Association of Independent Hardware Stores exists for conditions conducive to members' economic success for dues comparable to similar trade associations.

2.A. The top priority, deserving 50 percent of available resources, is that the general public recognizes and appreciates the benefits of shopping in independent hardware stores.

2.A.1. Members have a reputation for providing friendly advice to their customers.

2.A.2. Members' customers are confident that members have or can quickly get the items they seek.

2.B. Members have the ability and materials for effective self-promotion.

2.B.1. Members have a range of advertising copy.

2.B.2. Members know how to promote themselves through community projects.

2.C. Members can obtain inventory at favorable prices.

2.C.1. Members can obtain discounts when they purchase from selected suppliers.

2.D. Members have skills and tools crucial to business success.

> 2.D.1. Members have computer software that enables inventory management.

> 2.D.2. Small members have accounting and payroll skills.

> 2.D.3. Members have display and layout skills.

Policy Type: Ends

Policy Title: 1.0. Example F (Arts Council Ends Policies)

1. The Arts Council exists so that the people of Cultureville value and participate in the arts.

2.A. The people of Cultureville can learn about the arts from adequately funded providers.

> 2.A.1. People are aware of the link between arts and scholastic achievement.

> 2.A.2. Teachers are knowledgeable about the arts.

> 2.A.3. Learning about the arts is available to people of all ages—especially children under eighteen.

2.B. Arts organizations enjoy conditions conducive to their success.

> 2.B.1. Arts organizations have sufficient financial support.

> 2.B.2. Arts organizations benefit from cooperative marketing support.

> 2.B.3. Arts organizations' staff have necessary technical and managerial skills.

2.C. Artists live and work in a supportive environment.

> 2.C.1. Artistic achievement is encouraged and recognized.

> 2.C.2. Artists have the knowledge and information necessary for artistic and business success.

2.D. People value the role of the arts in society.

> 2.D.1. People value the arts' role in economic development.

> 2.D.2. People value the arts' role in community building.

> 2.D.3. The business community recognizes the role of the arts.

2.E. People participate in a broad range of arts activities.

> 2.E.1. Annual attendance at community arts events increases ____ percent per year.

> 2.E.2. Attendance at events is subsidized for those who cannot afford paid admissions.

Policy Type: Executive Limitations
Policy Title: 2.0. Global Executive Constraint

- The CEO shall not cause or allow any practice, activity, decision, or organizational circumstance that is unlawful, imprudent, or in violation of commonly accepted business and professional ethics and practices.

Note: This policy is the broadest of all policies in the Executive Limitations policy category and therefore the most open to interpretation. Any further Executive Limitations policies will merely be a narrowing of the provisions of this policy. The examples that follow demonstrate such further narrowing. Remember that the CEO is granted the authority to use *any reasonable interpretation* of the board's words.

Policy Type: Executive Limitations
Policy Title: 2.1. Treatment of Consumers

- With respect to interactions with consumers or those applying to be consumers, the CEO shall not cause or allow conditions, procedures, or decisions that are unsafe, untimely, undignified, or unnecessarily intrusive.

- Further, without limiting the scope of the foregoing by this enumeration, the CEO shall not

1. Elicit information for which there is no clear necessity

2. Use methods of collecting, reviewing, transmitting, or storing client information that fail to protect against improper access to the material elicited

3. Fail to operate facilities with appropriate accessibility and privacy

4. Fail to establish with consumers a clear understanding of what may be expected and what may not be expected from the service offered

5. Fail to inform consumers of this policy or to provide a way to be heard for persons who believe they have not been accorded a reasonable interpretation of their protections under this policy

Policy Type: Executive Limitations
Policy Title: 2.2. Treatment of Staff

- With respect to the treatment of paid and volunteer staff, the CEO shall not cause or allow conditions that are unfair, undignified, disorganized, or unclear.

- Further, without limiting the scope of the foregoing by this enumeration, the CEO shall not

1. Operate without written personnel rules that (a) clarify rules for staff, (b) provide for effective handling of grievances, and (c) protect against wrongful conditions, such as nepotism and grossly preferential treatment for personal reasons

2. Discriminate against any staff member for nondisruptive expression of dissent

3. Fail to acquaint staff with the CEO's interpretation of their protections under this policy

4. Allow staff to be unprepared to deal with emergency situations

Policy Type: Executive Limitations
Policy Title: 2.3. Financial Condition and Activities

- With respect to the actual, ongoing financial condition and activities, the CEO shall not cause or allow the development of financial jeopardy or material deviation of actual expenditures from board priorities established in Ends policies.

- Further, without limiting the scope of the foregoing by this enumeration, the CEO shall not

1. Expend more funds than have been received in the fiscal year to date unless the debt guideline (below) is met

2. Incur debt in an amount greater than can be repaid by certain otherwise unencumbered revenues within sixty days

3. Use any long-term reserves

4. Conduct interfund shifting in amounts greater than can be restored to a condition of discrete fund balances by certain otherwise unencumbered revenues within thirty days

5. Fail to settle payroll and debts in a timely manner

6. Allow tax payments or other government-ordered payments or filings to be overdue or inaccurately filed

7. Make a single purchase or commitment of greater than $_____. Splitting orders to avoid this limit is not acceptable.

8. Acquire, encumber, or dispose of real property

9. Fail to aggressively pursue receivables after a reasonable grace period

Policy Type: Executive Limitations
Policy Title: 2.4. Financial Planning and Budgeting

- The CEO shall not cause or allow financial planning for any fiscal year or the remaining part of any fiscal year to deviate materially from the board's Ends priorities, risk financial jeopardy, or fail to be derived from a multiyear plan.

- Further, without limiting the scope of the foregoing by this enumeration, there will be no financial plans that

1. Risk incurring those situations or conditions described as unacceptable in the board policy "Financial Condition and Activities"

2. Omit credible projection of revenues and expenses, separation of capital and operational items, cash flow, and disclosure of planning assumptions

3. Provide less for board prerogatives during the year than is set forth in the Governance Investment Policy

Policy Type: Executive Limitations
Policy Title: 2.5. Emergency CEO Succession

- To protect the board from sudden loss of CEO services, the CEO shall not permit there to be fewer than two other executives sufficiently familiar with board and CEO issues and processes to enable either to take over with reasonable proficiency as an interim successor.

Policy Type: Executive Limitations
Policy Title: 2.6. Asset Protection

- The CEO shall not cause or allow corporate assets to be unprotected, inadequately maintained, or unnecessarily risked.

- Further, without limiting the scope of the foregoing by this enumeration, the CEO shall not

1. Fail to insure against theft and casualty losses to at least 80 percent of replacement value and against liability losses to board members, staff, and the organization itself in an amount greater than the average for comparable organizations

2. Allow unbonded personnel access to material amounts of funds

3. Subject facilities and equipment to improper wear and tear or insufficient maintenance

4. Unnecessarily expose the organization, its board, or its staff to claims of liability

5. Make any purchase (a) wherein normally prudent protection has not been given against conflict of interest; (b) of over $_____ without having obtained comparative prices and quality; (c) of over $_____ without a stringent method of ensuring the balance of long-term quality and cost. Orders shall not be split to avoid these criteria.

6. Fail to protect intellectual property, information, and files from loss or significant damage

7. Receive, process, or disburse funds under controls that are insufficient to meet the board-appointed auditor's standards

8. Compromise the independence of the board's audit or other external monitoring or advice, such as by engaging parties already chosen by the board as consultants or advisers

9. Invest or hold operating capital in insecure instruments, including uninsured checking accounts and bonds of less than AA rating at any time, or in non-interest-bearing accounts except where necessary to facilitate ease in operational transactions

10. Endanger the organization's public image, its credibility, or its ability to accomplish ends

11. Change the organization's name or substantially alter its identity in the community

12. Create or purchase any subsidiary corporation unless (a) more than 80 percent is owned by this organization; (b) initial capitalization by this organization is less than $_____ or _____ percent of the reserve fund; (c) no staff member has an ownership interest; and (d) there is no reasonable chance of resultant damage to the reputation of this organization

Policy Type: Executive Limitations
Policy Title: 2.7. Compensation and Benefits

- With respect to employment, compensation, and benefits to employees, consultants, contract workers and volunteers, the CEO shall not cause or allow jeopardy to financial integrity or to public image.

- Further, without limiting the scope of the foregoing by this enumeration, the CEO shall not

1. Change the CEO's own compensation and benefits, except as his or her benefits are consistent with a package for all other employees

2. Promise or imply permanent or guaranteed employment

3. Establish current compensation and benefits that deviate materially from the geographical or professional market for the skills employed

4. Create obligations over a longer term than revenues can be safely projected, in no event longer than one year and in all events subject to losses in revenue

5. Establish or change pension benefits so as to cause unpredictable or inequitable situations, including those that

    A. Incur unfunded liabilities

    B. Provide less than some basic level of benefits to all full time employees, though differential benefits to encourage longevity are not prohibited

    C. Allow any employee to lose benefits already accrued from any previous plan

    D. Treat the CEO differently from other key employees

Policy Type: Executive Limitations
Policy Title: 2.8. Communication and Support to the Board

- The CEO shall not cause or allow the board to be uninformed or unsupported in its work.

- Further, without limiting the scope of the foregoing by this enumeration, the CEO shall not

1. Neglect to submit monitoring data required by the board (see policy 3.4 on monitoring CEO performance) in a timely, accurate, and understandable fashion, directly addressing the provisions of board policies being monitored

2. Fail to report in a timely manner any actual or anticipated noncompliance with any policy of the board

3. Neglect to submit unbiased decision information required periodically by the board or let the board be unaware of relevant trends

4. Let the board be unaware of any significant incidental information it requires, including anticipated media coverage, threatened or pending lawsuits, and material internal and external changes

5. Fail to advise the board if, in the CEO's opinion, the board is not in compliance with its own policies on Governance Process and Board-Management Delegation, particularly in the case of board behavior that is detrimental to the work relationship between the board and the CEO

6. Present information in unnecessarily complex or lengthy form or in a form that fails to differentiate among information of three types: monitoring, decision preparation, and other

7. Fail to provide a workable mechanism for official board, officer, or committee communications

8. Fail, when addressing official business, to deal with the board as a whole except when (a) fulfilling individual requests for information or (b) responding to officers or committees duly charged by the board

9. Fail to supply for the board's consent agenda, along with applicable monitoring information, all decisions delegated to the CEO yet required by law, regulation, or contract to be board-approved

Policy Type: Board-Management Delegation
Policy Title: 3.0. Global Governance-Management Connection

- The board's sole official connection to the operational organization, its achievements, and its conduct will be through a chief executive officer, titled _____.

Policy Type: Board-Management Delegation
Policy Title: 3.1. Unity of Control

- Only officially passed motions of the board are binding on the CEO.

- Accordingly:

1. Decisions or instructions of individual board members, officers, or committees are not binding on the CEO except in rare instances when the board has specifically authorized such exercise of authority.

2. In the case of board members or committees requesting information or assistance without board authorization, the CEO can refuse such requests that require, in the CEO's opinion, a material amount of staff time or funds or is disruptive.

Policy Type: Board-Management Delegation
Policy Title: 3.2. Accountability of the CEO

- The CEO is the board's only link to operational achievement and conduct, so that all authority and accountability of staff, as far as the board is concerned, is considered the authority and accountability of the CEO.

- Accordingly:

1. The board will never give instructions to persons who report directly or indirectly to the CEO.

2. The board will not evaluate, either formally or informally, any staff other than the CEO.

3. The board will view CEO performance as identical to organizational performance so that organizational accomplishment of board-stated ends and avoidance of board-proscribed means will be viewed as successful CEO performance.

Policy Type: Board-Management Delegation
Policy Title: 3.3. Delegation to the CEO

- The board will instruct the CEO through written policies that prescribe the organizational ends to be achieved and describe organizational situations and actions to be avoided, allowing the CEO to use any reasonable interpretation of these policies.

- Accordingly:

1. The board will develop policies instructing the CEO to achieve specified results for specified recipients at a specified cost. These policies will be developed systematically from the broadest, most general level to more defined levels and will be called Ends policies. All issues that are not ends issues as defined here are means issues.

2. The board will develop policies that limit the latitude the CEO may exercise in choosing the organizational means. These policies will be developed systematically from the broadest, most general level to more defined levels, and they will be called Executive Limitations policies. The board will never prescribe organizational means delegated to the CEO.

3. As long as the CEO uses *any reasonable interpretation* of the board's Ends and Executive Limitations policies, the CEO is authorized to establish all further policies, make all decisions, take all actions, establish all practices, and pursue all activities. Such decisions of the CEO shall have full force and authority as if decided by the board.

4. The board may change its Ends and Executive Limitations policies, thereby shifting the boundary between board and CEO domains. By doing so, the board changes the latitude of choice given to the CEO. But as long as any particular delegation is in place, the board will respect and support the CEO's choices.

Policy Type: Board-Management Delegation
Policy Title: 3.4. Monitoring CEO Performance

- Systematic and rigorous monitoring of CEO job performance will be solely against the only expected CEO job outputs: organizational accomplishment of board policies on ends and organizational operation within the boundaries established in board policies on Executive Limitations.

- Accordingly:

1. Monitoring is simply to determine the degree to which board policies are being met. Information that does not do this will not be considered to be monitoring information.

2. The board will acquire monitoring information by one or more of three methods: (a) by internal report, in which the CEO discloses interpretations and compliance information to the board; (b) by external report, in which an external, disinterested third party selected by the board assesses compliance with board policies; or (c) by direct board inspection, in which a designated member or members of the board assess compliance with the appropriate policy criteria.

3. In every case, the board will judge (a) the reasonableness of the CEO's interpretation and (b) whether data demonstrate accomplishment of the interpretation.

4. In every case, the standard for compliance shall be *any reasonable CEO interpretation* of the board policy being monitored. The board is the final arbiter of reasonableness but will always judge with a "reasonable person" test rather than with interpretations favored by board members or by the board as a whole.

5. All policies that instruct the CEO will be monitored at a frequency and by a method chosen by the board. The board can monitor any policy at any time by any method but will ordinarily depend on a routine schedule.

Policy	Method	Frequency	Month
Ends	Internal	Annually	Feb.
Global Executive Constraint	Internal	Annually	Mar.
Treatment of Consumers	Internal	Annually	May
Treatment of Staff	Internal	Annually	May

Policy	Method	Frequency	Month
Financial Condition and Activities	Internal	Quarterly	Jan., Apr., July, Oct.
	External	Annually	Sept.
Financial Planning and Budgeting	Internal	Quarterly	Feb., May, Aug., Nov.
Emergency CEO Succession	Internal	Annually	Oct.
Asset Protection	Internal	Annually	Nov.
Compensation and Benefits	Internal	Annually	Nov.
	External	Biannually	Sept. of odd-numbered years
Communication and Support	Direct inspection	Annually	July

Policy Type: Governance Process
Policy Title: 4.0. Global Governance Commitment

- The purpose of the board, on behalf of [identify the ownership here], is to see to it that [name of organization here] (a) achieves appropriate results for appropriate persons at an appropriate cost (as specified in board Ends policies) and (b) avoids unacceptable actions and situations (as prohibited in board Executive Limitations policies).

Note: The "moral ownership" identity is to be inserted in the blank provided. This could be "the general public," "the people of Montgomery County," "the membership," "the citizens of San Francisco," or other such base of ownership.

Policy Type: Governance Process
Policy Title: 4.1. Governing Style

- The board will govern lawfully, observing the principles of the Policy Governance model, with an emphasis on (a) outward vision rather than an internal preoccupation, (b) encouragement of diversity in viewpoints, (c) strategic leadership more than administrative detail, (d) clear distinction of board and chief executive roles, (e) collective rather than individual decisions, (f) future rather than past or present, and (g) proactivity rather than reactivity.

- Accordingly:

1. The board will cultivate a sense of group responsibility. The board, not the staff, will be responsible for excellence in governing. The board will be the initiator of policy, not merely a reactor to staff initiatives. The board will not use the expertise of individual members to substitute for the judgment of the board, although the expertise of individual members may be used to enhance the understanding of the board as a body.

2. The board will direct, control, and inspire the organization through the careful establishment of broad written policies reflecting the board's values and perspectives. The board's major policy focus will be on the intended long-term impacts outside the staff organization, not on the administrative or programmatic means of attaining those effects.

3. The board will enforce upon itself whatever discipline is needed to govern with excellence. Discipline will apply to matters such as attendance, preparation for meetings, policymaking principles, respect of roles, and ensuring the continuance of governance capability. Although the board can change its Governance Process policies at any time, it will scrupulously observe those currently in force.

4. Continual board development will include orientation of new board members in the board's Governance Process and periodic board discussion of process improvement.

5. The board will allow no officer, individual, or committee of the board to hinder or serve as an excuse for not fulfilling group obligations.

6. The board will monitor and discuss the board's process and performance at each meeting. Self-monitoring will include comparison of board activity and discipline to policies in the Governance Process and Board-Management Delegation categories.

Policy Type: Governance Process
Policy Title: 4.2. Board Job Products

- Specific job outputs of the board, as an informed agent of the ownership, are those that ensure appropriate organizational performance.

- Accordingly, the board has direct responsibility to create

1. The linkage between the ownership and the operational organization

2. Written governing policies that realistically address the broadest levels of all organizational decisions and situations

A. Ends: organizational products, impacts, benefits, outcomes, recipients, and their relative worth (what good for which recipients at what cost)

B. Executive limitations: constraints on executive authority that establish the prudence and ethics boundaries within which all executive activity and decisions must take place

C. Governance process: specification of how the board conceives, carries out, and monitors its own task

D. Board-management delegation: how power is delegated and its proper use; the CEO's role, authority, and accountability

3. Assurance of successful organizational performance on Ends and Executive Limitations.

Note: A board can set annual targets about integrity or completeness in these areas either by expanding this policy or establishing a separate policy titled, for example, "annual governance plan." Other job "products" of the board that may be appropriate for some organizations may include "legislative change," "donor funding," or other outputs for which the board chooses to hold itself directly responsible. Be sure to include any decision areas that Executive Limitations policies have denied to the CEO.

Policy Type: Governance Process
Policy Title: 4.3. Agenda Planning

- To accomplish its job products with a governance style consistent with board policies, the board will follow an annual agenda that (a) completes a reexploration of Ends policies annually and (b) continually improves board performance through board education and enriched input and deliberation.

1. The cycle will conclude each year on the last day of September so that administrative planning and budgeting can be based on accomplishing a one-year segment of the board's most recent statement of long-term ends.

2. The cycle will start with the board's development of its agenda for the next year.

A. Consultations with selected groups in the ownership, or other methods of gaining ownership input, will be determined and arranged in the first quarter, to be held during the balance of the year.

B. Governance education and education related to ends determination (presentations by futurists, demographers, advocacy groups, staff, and so on) will be arranged in the first quarter, to be held during the balance of the year.

    C. A board member may recommend or request an item for board discussion by submitting the item to the CGO no later than five days before the board meeting.

3. Throughout the year, the board will attend to consent agenda items as expeditiously as possible.

4. CEO monitoring will be included on the agenda if monitoring reports show policy violations, if policy criteria are to be debated, or if the board, for any reason, chooses to debate amending its monitoring schedule.

5. CEO remuneration will be decided after a review of monitoring reports received in the last year during the month of February.

Policy Type: Governance Process
Policy Title: 4.4. Chief Governance Officer's Role

- The chief governance officer (CGO), a specially empowered member of the board, ensures the integrity of the board's process and, secondarily, occasionally represents the board to outside parties.

- Accordingly:

1. The assigned result of the CGO's job is that the board behaves consistently with its own rules and those legitimately imposed on it from outside the organization.

    A. Meeting discussion content will consist solely of issues that clearly belong to the board to decide or to monitor according to board policy.

    B. Information that is for neither monitoring performance nor board decisions will be avoided or minimized and always noted as such.

    C. Deliberation will be fair, open, and thorough but also timely, orderly, and kept to the point.

2. The authority of the CGO consists in making decisions that fall within topics covered by board policies on Governance Process and Board-Management Delegation, with the exception of (a) employment or termination of a CEO and (b) areas where the board specifically delegates portions of this authority to others. The CGO is authorized to use any reasonable interpretation of the provisions in these policies.

    A. The CGO is empowered to chair board meetings with all the commonly accepted powers of that position, such as ruling and recognizing.

B. The CGO has no authority to make decisions about policies created by the board within Ends and Executive Limitations policy areas. Therefore, the CGO has no authority to supervise or direct the CEO.

C. The CGO may represent the board to outside parties in announcing board-stated positions and in stating chair decisions and interpretations within the area delegated to her or him.

D. The CGO may delegate this authority but remains accountable for its use.

Policy Type: Governance Process
Policy Title: 4.5. Board Members' Code of Conduct

- The board commits itself and its members to ethical, businesslike, and lawful conduct, including proper use of authority and appropriate decorum when acting as board members.

1. Members must demonstrate loyalty to the ownership, unconflicted by loyalties to staff, other organizations, or any personal interests as consumers.

2. Members must avoid conflict of interest with respect to their fiduciary responsibility.

   A. There will be no self-dealing or business by a member with the organization. Members will annually disclose their involvements with other organizations or with vendors and any associations that might be reasonably seen as representing a conflict of interest.

   B. When the board is to decide on an issue about which a member has an unavoidable conflict of interest, that member shall absent herself or himself without comment not only from the vote but also from the deliberation.

   C. Board members will not use their board position to obtain employment in the organization for themselves, family members, or close associates. A board member who applies for employment must first resign from the board.

3. Board members may not attempt to exercise individual authority over the organization.

   A. Members' interaction with the CEO or with staff must recognize the lack of authority vested in individuals except when explicitly authorized by the board.

    B. Members' interactions with the public, the press, or other entities must recognize the same limitation and the inability of any board member to speak for the board except to repeat explicitly stated board decisions.

    C. Except for participation in board deliberation about whether the CEO has achieved any reasonable interpretation of board policy, members will not express individual judgments of performance of employees or the CEO.

4. Members will respect the confidentiality appropriate to issues of a sensitive nature.

5. Members will be properly prepared for board deliberation.

6. Members will support the legitimacy and authority of the final determination of the board on any matter, irrespective of the member's personal position on the issue.

7. Members will contribute [no less than $_____][no fewer than _____ hours as operational volunteers as directed by staff] each year.

Policy Type: Governance Process
Policy Title: 4.6. Board Committee Principles

- Board committees, when used, will be assigned so as to reinforce the wholeness of the board's job and so as never to interfere with delegation from board to CEO.

- Accordingly:

1. Board committees are to help the board do its job, not to help or advise the staff. Committees ordinarily will assist the board by preparing policy alternatives and implications for board deliberation. In keeping with the board's broader focus, board committees will normally not have direct dealings with current staff operations.

2. Board committees may not speak or act for the board except when formally given such authority for specific and time-limited purposes. Expectations and authority will be carefully stated in order not to conflict with authority delegated to the CEO.

3. Board committees cannot exercise authority over staff. Because the CEO works for the full board, he or she will not be required to obtain the approval of a board committee before an executive action.

4. Board committees are to avoid overidentification with organizational parts rather than the whole. Therefore, a board committee that has

helped the board create policy on some topic will not be used to monitor organizational performance on that same subject.

5. Committees will be used sparingly and ordinarily in an ad hoc capacity.

6. This policy applies to any group that is formed by board action, whether or not it is called a committee and regardless of whether the group includes board members. It does not apply to committees formed under the authority of the CEO.

Policy Type: Governance Process
Policy Title: 4.7. Board Committee Structure

• A committee is a board committee only if its existence and charge come from the board, regardless of whether board members sit on the committee. The only board committees are those that are set forth in this policy. Unless otherwise stated, a committee ceases to exist as soon as its task is complete.

Note: This is *not* a list of suggested committees but rather an illustration of how legitimate board committees should be described.

1. Ownership Linkages Committee

   A. *Product:* Options and implications for board consideration with respect to the ends decisions to be made by the board regarding the needs of disabled persons—by no later than August 15, 200X.

   B. *Authority:* To incur costs of no more than $1,000 in direct charges and no more than fifty hours of staff time.

2. Legislative Change Advisory Committee

   A. *Product:* Options and implications for board consideration regarding long-term legislative or regulatory effects to be achieved by the board—by no later than September 30, 200X.

   B. *Authority:* To incur costs of no more than $3,000 in direct charges and no more than seventy hours of staff time.

3. Nominating Committee

   A. *Product:* Properly screened potential board members—by no later than May 20 of each year.

   B. *Authority:* To incur costs of no more than $1,000 in direct charges and no more than twenty hours of staff time per annum.

4. Audit Committee

   A. *Product:* Specification of scope of audit prior to outside audit—by no later than January 10 of each year.

B. *Authority:* To incur no more than $30,000 in direct charges and use of no more than fifty person-hours of staff time per annum.

Policy Type: Governance Process
Policy Title: 4.8. Governance Investment

- Because poor governance costs more than learning to govern well, the board will invest in its governance capacity.

- Accordingly:

1. Board skills, methods, and supports will be sufficient to ensure governing with excellence.

    A. Training and retraining will be used liberally to orient new members and candidates for membership, as well as to maintain and increase existing member skills and understandings.

    B. Outside monitoring assistance will be arranged so that the board can exercise confident control over organizational performance. This includes, but is not limited to, financial audits.

    C. Outreach mechanisms will be used as needed to ensure the board's ability to listen to owner viewpoints and values.

2. Costs will be prudently incurred, though not at the expense of endangering the development and maintenance of superior capability.

    A. Up to $_____ in fiscal year _____ for training, including attendance at conferences and workshops.

    B. Up to $_____ in fiscal year _____ for auditing and other third-party monitoring of organizational performance.

    C. Up to $_____ in fiscal year _____ for surveys, focus groups, opinion analyses, and meeting costs.

3. The board will establish its cost of governance budget for the next fiscal year during the month of October.

Resource 4
Further Reading

Carver, J. *Boards That Make a Difference: A New Design for Leadership in Nonprofit and Public Organizations.* (2nd ed.) San Francisco: Jossey-Bass, 1997.

Carver, J. *The Unique Double Servant-Leadership Role of the Board Chairperson.* Voices of Servant-Leadership Series, no. 2. Indianapolis, Ind.: Greenleaf Center for Servant-Leadership, 1999.

Carver, J. *John Carver on Board Leadership: Selected Writings from the Creator of the World's Most Provocative and Systematic Governance Model.* San Francisco: Jossey-Bass, 2001.

Carver, J., and Carver, M. M. *The CarverGuide Series on Effective Board Governance,* nos. 1–12. San Francisco: Jossey-Bass, 1996–1997.

Carver, J., and Carver, M. M. *Reinventing Your Board: A Step-by-Step Guide to Implementing Policy Governance.* San Francisco: Jossey-Bass, 1997.

Carver, J., with Oliver, C. *Corporate Boards That Create Value.* San Francisco: Jossey-Bass, 2002.

Greenleaf, R. K. *Servant Leadership: A Journey into the Nature of Legitimate Power and Greatness.* New York: Paulist Press, 1977.

How to Use
the Accompanying CD-ROM

System Requirements

PC with Microsoft Windows 98SE or later

Mac with Apple OS version 8.6 or later

Using the CD with Windows

To view the items located on the CD, follow these steps:

1. Insert the CD into your computer's CD-ROM drive.

2. After you click "Accept" on the end user's license agreement and copyright information window, a window appears with the following options you can click on:

   Contents: Allows you to view the files included on the CD.

   Software: Allows you to install useful software from the CD.

   Links: Displays hyperlinked Web sites.

   Authors: Displays information about the authors.

   Contact Us: Displays information on contacting the publisher or authors.

   Help: Displays information on using the CD.

   Exit: Closes the interface window.

If you do not have autorun enabled, or if the autorun window does not appear, follow these steps to access the CD:

1. Click Start, then Run.

2. In the dialog box that appears, type d:\start.exe, where d is the letter of your CD-ROM drive. This brings up the autorun window described in the preceding set of steps.

3. Choose the desired option from the menu.

In Case of Trouble

If you experience difficulty using the CD, please follow these steps:

1. Make sure your hardware and systems configurations conform to the systems requirements noted under System Requirements above.

2. Review the installation procedure for your type of hardware and operating system. It is possible to reinstall the software if necessary.

To speak with someone in Product Technical Support, call 800-762–2974 or 317–572–3994 M-F 8:30 A.M.—5:00 P.M. EST. You can also get support and contact Product Technical Support at http://www.wiley.com/techsupport.

Before calling or writing, please have the following information available:

- Type of computer and operating system
- Any error messages displayed
- Complete description of the problem.

It is best if you are sitting at your computer when making the call.